...ng director, the curricu-
...ue interested in more effec-
...ethods will gain new insights
...earning fr... the five carefully
...h stu... ... the free ex-
well known

A PUBLICATION OF

THE FOUNDATION for RESEARCH on HUMAN BEHAVIOR

PROGRAMED

LEARNING:

A CRITICAL

EVALUATION

J. L. HUGHES, *Editor*

EDUCATIONAL METHODS, Inc. / *Chicago, Illinois*

Library of Congress Catalog Card Number 63-21734

Copyright © 1963 by the
Foundation for Research on Human Behavior

First published 1963 by

Educational Methods, Inc.
A Subsidiary of Aldine Publishing Company
64 East Van Buren St.
Chicago, Illinois 60605

Designed by David Miller
Printed in the United States of America

Second Printing

CONTENTS

PREFACE

In October, 1960, the Foundation for Research on Human Behavior sponsored a two-day meeting at Rochester, New York, for the purpose of examining the then emerging field of programed learning and considering the implications of this technique for industrial training. The meeting was planned in collaboration with representatives from the Eastman Kodak Company and International Business Machines Corporation, two member companies of the Foundation which were active in the field at the time. Three psychologists, well known for their contributions to programed learning, presented papers describing basic principles and theoretical concepts in this field, and a number of industrial psychologists and industrial training executives described the results of preliminary efforts to apply programed learning in industrial training situations. Because the proceedings appeared to be of general interest to those working in programed learning, a record of the meeting was later published.*

Encouraged by the success of the first meeting, the Foundation proposed a second two-day seminar for the spring of 1962. By this time, more experimental data on programed learning had accumulated as a result of a number

* Programmed Learning: Evolving Principles and Industrial Applications. J. P. Lysaught, Editor. The Foundation for Research on Human Behavior, Ann Arbor, Michigan, 1961.

of academic and industrial studies. Persons active in the field were thus in a better position to evaluate its effectiveness and consider the implications of this technique for industrial training.

The structure of the seminar called for a number of industrial psychologists and training executives to present the results of studies conducted in their organizations. After each paper, a discussant noted for his contributions to learning theory and/or programed learning commented on the significant theoretical and practical issues raised and suggested areas for future research. Following the presentation of the paper and the discussant's comments, the meeting was thrown open to questions and general discussion. Attending the seminar were representatives from a number of companies and other organizations interested in programed learning. The result was a free interchange of ideas from participants with varying backgrounds—education, experimental psychology, industrial psychology, and industrial training.

Much has been made of the failure of communication between educators and experimental psychologists on the one hand, and industrial training people on the other. This seminar represented an attempt to break down some of the barriers and provide for a cross-fertilization of ideas from these different quarters. It was felt that if the results of typical industrial training studies were presented, the ensuing comments by experimental psychologists would produce suggestions for improving the rigor of industrial research and would stimulate future research efforts. In turn, it was anticipated that these psychologists would acquire a better understanding of some of the practical training problems encountered in industry and the difficulties of doing research in this environment.

The chairman of the seminar was Dr. Walter J. McNamara, Manager of Applied Personnel Research, International Business Machines Corporation, the host company for the meeting. Arrangements for the seminar represented the efforts and suggestions of Dr. Sven Lundstedt and Dr. Hollis W. Peter of the Foundation, Dr. Robert Glaser of the University of Pittsburgh, and Dr. McNamara and Dr. J. L. Hughes of IBM. The speakers, discussants, and participants were as follows:

SPEAKERS AND DISCUSSANTS

- James S. Bruce, Director of Training, Eastman Kodak Company
- Dr. James Deese, Professor of Psychology, The Johns Hopkins University
- Dr. Robert M. Gagne, Director of Research, American Institute for Research
- Dr. Robert Glaser, Professor of Psychology, University of Pittsburgh
- Dr. Howard O. Holt, Director of Training Research, American Telephone and Telegraph Company
- Dr. John L. Hughes, Consultant, Education Research, International Business Machines Corporation

Richard J. Morse, Instructional Methods Administrator, General Telephone Company of California

Lawrence H. O'Donnell, Consultant, Engineering Service Division, E. I. duPont de Nemours and Company

PARTICIPANTS

Edward Beck, Personnel Research Supervisor, Bell Telephone Company of Pennsylvania

John T. Childs, Manager of Programed Instruction, Equitable Life Assurance Society of the U.S.

Dr. Donald Cook, Director of Programing, Basic Systems Incorporated

Laurence T. Deabler, Manager, Education Processes, International Business Machine Corporation

John E. Hay, Staff Psychologist, Personnel Research Division, Sun Oil Company

Harry D. Kolb, Manager, Personnel Development, Humble Oil and Refining Company

Richard Knight, Training Department, Eastman Kodak Company

Dr. Harry Laurent, Social Science Research Advisor, Standard Oil Company (New Jersey)

Dr. Sven Lundstedt, Assistant Director, Foundation for Research on Human Behavior

Dr. Hollis W. Peter, Director, Foundation for Research on Human Behavior

Robert J. Seidel, Research Scientist, HumRRO

Gordon S. Watts, Supervisor of Training, Corning Glass Works

R. A. Whitehorne, Manager, Personnel Research and Services, International Business Machines Corporation

Mrs. Aldo Williamson, Assistant to the Vice President, United Parcel Service

The seminar turned out to be a rewarding one for the participants during which many of the critical issues in programed learning were presented, discussed and evaluated. For this reason, it was decided to publish the papers presented and a transcript of the subsequent discussions. The following pages constitute this report.

J. L. HUGHES,
Editor

White Plains, New York

PROGRAMED LEARNING:

A Critical Evaluation

I

AN EXPLORATORY STUDY OF THE
USE OF A SELF-INSTRUCTION PROGRAM IN
BASIC ELECTRICITY *

H . O . H O L T

BACKGROUND

The study I am about to describe was undertaken by the Communications Social Science Research Department of the Bell Telephone Laboratories. It is exploratory in nature and was designed to provide us a close working acquaintance with problems of programing and to yield an estimate of the effectiveness of a self-instruction program

* This talk is based upon a report of the same title by H. O. Holt, Bell Telephone Laboratories, and C. G. Valentine, Michigan Bell Telephone Company, released in mimeographed form by the Bell Telephone Laboratories, Murray Hill, N. J.

Many persons in the Bell System helped to make this study possible through their cooperation. In addition, special thanks are due Dr. Ira H. Cisin, consultant, for his help throughout the project; Dr. Myron Woolman, contractor, for his participation in the planning of the experimental study as well as for his programing contributions noted elsewhere in this report; Dr. Joseph Hammock, Bell Telephone Laboratories, for valuable suggestions; and Miss H. P. Reagan, Bell Telephone Laboratories, who handled production of the program and performed much of the computation of data.

15

relative to the traditional lecture-discussion method of in-struction. Since most "teaching machine" research performed up to the time this study was started was done in nonstandard instructional settings with very short programs using subjects of high general ability, the present study was designed to yield results which would be more indicative of what could be expected in the normal instructional situation. Hence a long course was selected for programing (approximately 54 class-room hours); the experimental classes were conducted by regular instructors in the usual classroom, and the range of subjects' IQs was from 92 to 122 with a mean of 107.

The subject matter selected for programing was basic electricity. It was decided that the program would be written to match as closely as possible the content of an ongoing course. The ultimate end of the study was a comparative estimate of efficiency of the two types of courses. The basic electricity course of a nearby operating telephone company was selected, partly because of the proximity of its plant school to the Bell Telephone Laboratories and partly be-cause the course was taught entirely by lectures and films. Comparing the program with such a course was felt to be less complicated than comparing it with a course that made extensive use of laboratory exercises and demonstrations. The selected course normally was taught with the lecture-discussion method in a period of nine six-hour days.

Two obvious requirements had to be met before the experiment could be undertaken: a program of instruction had to be written, and decisions had to be made about mode of presentation of the program to students. A team was formed to undertake the construction of the program. Its members provided the two types of experience thought necessary: skill in the art of programing, and detailed knowledge of the subject matter to be programed.[1] Under the constraint that it had to match the contents of the lecture-discussion course, the final program possesses the following features:

1. The program is linear in type. Branching in the usual sense is not used, although two different kinds of treatment are provided: (a) periodic diagnostic tests are administered and trainees repeat sections that are inadequately mastered; and (b) faster students may work additional sets of practice problems.

2. Responses are written directly on the tape or page; the student fills in the missing part of each statement in context.

3. The learner is expected to construct his response. However, he has an answer list of some 30 terms in front of him at all times against which he may check his response.

4. Panel illustrations are used to supplement the teaching program. Thus, an item in the program can be keyed to an illustration that is displayed separately to the student.

5. The instructor is not completely eliminated.

1. Dr. Myron Woolman, then with the Human Resources Research Office, now Director of The Institute of Educational Research, Inc., Washington, D. C., and Mr. C. G. Valentine, now with Michigan Bell Telephone Company.

Because of the wide variety of trainees' ability and previous experience, it would be impractical to write a program employing a level of discourse appropriate to the least qualified student. Therefore, the instructor is permitted to offer individual help to those students who have difficulty understanding a part of the program or whose background is insufficient.

The requirements placed upon the mode of presentation grew partly out of decisions that were made with regard to programing philosophy, as discussed above. In addition, the mode of presentation had to lend itself to a printing method and a teaching machine system that would meet the following requirements:

1. The machine had to be cheat-proof, so that a response made by the student could not be altered.

2. The frame, response blank, and confirming response had to be presented in such a location that they would be easily readable; and the writing surface had to be located so that the learner could assume a natural position.

3. The machine had to provide a continuous flow of items for several hours without interruptions due to changing of sheets, reloading the machine, or other such factors.

4. The printing method had to provide for a high degree of flexibility during the program revision period so that items could be added, deleted or changed without disturbing the balance of the program.

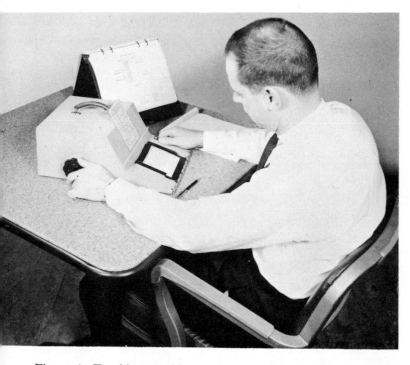

Figure 1. Teaching machine and associated panel book in use.

Since none of the available machines met these requirements, a new printing and teaching machine system was
developed at the Laboratories.[2] The teaching machine is
pictured in Figures 1 and 2, and the printer, a modified
Elliott Addressing Machine, is pictured in Figure 3. The
program is printed on five-inch rolls of paper tape which
may be up to 225 feet in length.

2. Mr. John B. Gilpin, a technical aide, Bell Telephone Laboratories,
Incorporated, now Research Associate, UICSM Mathematics Project, University of Illinois, Urbana, Illinois, was primarily responsible for the
design of the machine and for aspects of the printing process.

Figure 2. Teaching machine open for loading of paper tape.

Figure 3. Elliott Addressing Machine modified
to print on five-inch paper tape.

PILOT STUDIES

Two small-group pilot studies and a large field pilot study were run before the program was used in the controlled experiment which had been planned. As a result of the pilot studies, the program underwent two major revisions and a minor revision. The final version contains 2,505 items and calls for a total of 3,500 separate responses. It is divided into twelve units. Nine diagnostic tests or end-of-unit quizzes are employed. In addition, several auxiliary devices were added to the program as a result of the pilot studies:

1. A laminated card containing most of the basic terms, units, codes and formulas used in the course.

2. A set of summary notes covering the entire program.

3. Tables of sine function values and of square roots.

4. Four sets of practice problems primarily intended for the faster students to work in class.

5. Circuit solution guides to help those students who had trouble in solving complex R circuits and AC circuits.

6. A guide for use by instructors containing instructions on how to conduct the self-instruction course together with a rationale for the programing techniques.

It was possible to incorporate a study of mode of program presentation into the field pilot study. Each class was divided randomly and half the trainees completed the program presented by teaching machines while the other half worked through the program presented in booklet form. (Figure 4 shows the type of programed booklet used in the study.) The

Figure 4. Programed booklet and associated panel book in use.

results of this comparison have been reported elsewhere.[3]

THE EXPERIMENTAL STUDY

Soon after completion of the field pilot study it became possible at the selected telephone company plant school to stage the type of experiment that had been planned in which the same kinds of men could be divided into two groups: one taught by the standard lecture-discussion method (C) and the other by the self-instruction method (X). The primary objective of this study was to compare the effects of method C and method X on the proficiency of telephone technicians being trained in basic electricity. Scores on two criterion measures taken immediately after training were to constitute the main bases for comparison. In addition, retention would be measured by tests given six months after completion of training. These tests consisted of the following:

1. A "facts" examination. This test is a conventional achievement test consisting of 75 multiple choice and completion items. One form of the test was administered immediately after training; an equivalent form was administered six months later.

2. A "concepts" examination. This test is designed to measure the trainees' ability to manipulate

---

3. No significant differences were found between the book and machine treatments, either in proficiency or time. See Holt, Howard O. and Hammock, Joseph. Books as teaching machines: some data. In S. Margulies and L. D. Eigen (Eds.), *Applied Programed Instruction*. New York: John Wiley & Sons, 1962, pp. 50-56.

electrical concepts. It consists of specially constructed items of the "situational" type, each of which requires several responses. Only one form of this test was available and it was administered on both occasions.

In addition to, or sometimes in lieu of, gains in proficiency, programed self-instruction is alleged to result in savings in average training time. Thus "time for completion" records were maintained in all X classes in order to compare methods C and X with regard to time. Method C, of course, had a fixed time for completion whereas method X had variable times for completion since the self-instruction program is self-paced.

Two secondary notions were investigated:

1. Because the self-instruction program calls for a great deal of careful reading, it was hypothesized that there might be a significant improvement in reading skill among the trainees in the X group. To test this hypothesis, the Davis Reading Test was administered both before and after training.

2. Again, as in the field pilot study, trainees in the X classes were divided randomly, half the men worked through the program in teaching machines, while the other half worked through the same program in booklet form. This difference in treatment would yield further data on the relative effectiveness of the machine and programed book modes of presentation.

Ideally, this kind of experiment calls for classes assigned to the two methods to be trained simultaneously, but the input of trainees at the plant school was insufficient for simultaneous treatment. Nor was it possible to assign men strictly randomly to the two instructional methods; instead it was necessary that the experiment be staged in tandem: first a group of men (several classes) would be trained by the standard method; then a comparable group would be trained by the self-instruction method. This procedure involves an assumption that variation in input characteristics is nonbiasing across fairly short periods of time, an assumption that is not unreasonable. In addition, prior to training, measures of background variables were made on all trainees, so that the C and X groups could be equated statistically if they turned out to differ significantly. The measures were of:

1. Intelligence. The Otis Employment Test, Form B, was used.

2. Preknowledge of basic electricity. A completion-type test was used consisting of 45 critical items selected from the program by the programing team.

3. Years of company service (Bell System). This information was extracted from a short questionnaire completed by each trainee.

4. Semesters of mathematics and electricity training taken prior to the experiment. This information was taken from the trainee questionnaire.

A different instructor (selected by the plant school) was assigned to each method. Since self-instruction classes do not have an instructor in the usual sense, any biasing effect of having one instructor for the conventional classes and another instructor for the self-instruction classes was felt to be unimportant.

The classes were conducted in a regular classroom in the plant school. The school day was six hours in length, and men in the C method attended classes on ten successive workdays. One additional day was added to the standard course to allow time for testing. Men in the X method attended as many days as were necessary for them to complete the program and the testing.[4] On the opening day, all classes were met by the regular instructor and a Bell Telephone Laboratories experimenter. Men in both treatments were informed as to the nature of the experiment in which they were involved. The Bell Laboratories representative administered all pretests. It was felt that while little could be done to counteract the "Hawthorne" or special treatment effects in the X method classes, this special treatment of the C classes might serve to induce some Hawthorne effect in those classes and serve to make them more nearly equal to the others in this respect.

4. Thirty-eight trainees started the program in the X classes. Thirty-five completed the entire course. One of the thirty-five men was found to have taken the basic electricity course within the past year and was, therefore, disqualified. Of the three men who dropped out, two had contracted contagious diseases, while the third was a low aptitude man who was unable to complete the course within the arbitrary time limit of fourteen working days.

The sequence of events in all classes was as follows:

TABLE 1

Experimental Design

Treatment	C N=30	X N=34
Pretraining:		
Questionnaire	√	√
Otis Employment Test, Form B	√	√
Electrical Preknowledge Test	√	√
Davis Reading Test 1B	√	√
Training:		
Lecture-discussion (C)	√	No
Self-instruction (X)	No	√
Immediate Posttraining:		
Facts Examination (Form I)	√	√
Concepts Examination	√	√
Davis Reading Test 1A	√	√
6-months Posttraining:		
Facts Examination (Form II)	√	√
Concepts Examination	√	√

RESULTS

Control Variables

As was stated earlier, measures of intelligence, pre-knowledge of electricity, semesters of mathematics and electricity taken before training, and years of company service were taken prior to training so that the C and X groups could be equated statistically if they turned out to differ significantly. Figure 5 summarizes these control variables. There are no significant differences between groups on any

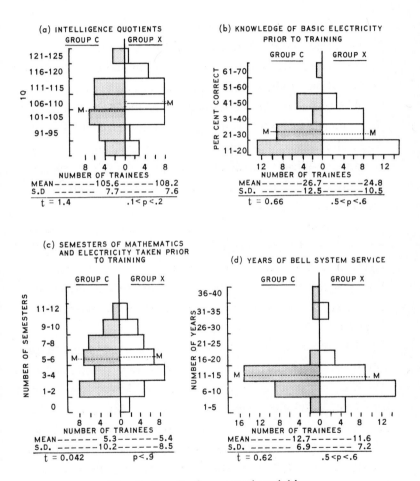

Fig. 5. Results for control variables.

of the four variables, and the C and X groups, therefore, are considered equivalent for the purposes of this study.

Criterion Variables

Proficiency in basic electricity·was measured immediately after completion of training and again six months later. The two tests used were the Facts Examination and the Concepts Examination; both of which were described earlier.

The results of the administration of the Facts Examination immediately after training are summarized in Fig. 6. The difference between mean scores of the C and X groups is highly significant statistically in favor of the self-instruction (X) group. All but five scores in the X group are above the mean of the C group.

The results of the administration of the Concepts Examination immediately after training are summarized in Fig. 7. Again, the difference between means of the two groups is highly significant statistically in favor of the self-instruction group. All scores in the X group are above the mean of the C group.

The other main criterion variable is time required to complete the course. Accurate records were maintained in the X classes of all time spent by men on the self-instruction program. Total classroom time for the C classes was fixed. The comparison between the two groups is inaccurate, however, because administrative restrictions made it impossible to get an estimate of time spent by members of the C classes in home study. (It is fairly well established that men in the

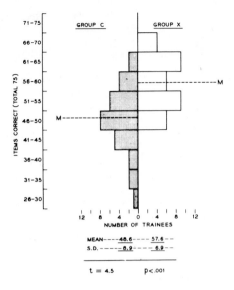

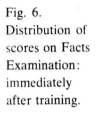

Fig. 6.
Distribution of
scores on Facts
Examination:
immediately
after training.

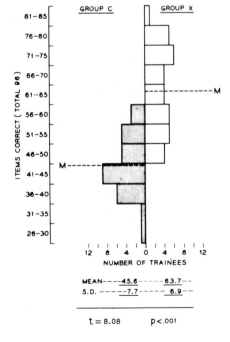

Fig. 7.
Distribution of
scores on
Concepts Examination:
immediately
after training.

X classes did not do home study since they were not given any study materials.) The only accurate comparison that can be made, therefore, is with regard to the average time spent *in the classroom* by the two groups. Those data are summarized in Fig. 8 which shows the mean classroom time of the two groups to be almost identical.

Self-pacing is an inherent characteristic of programed self-instruction. The result, of course, is that trainees using that method take different lengths of time to complete the course. Figure 8 shows a spread of finishing times among

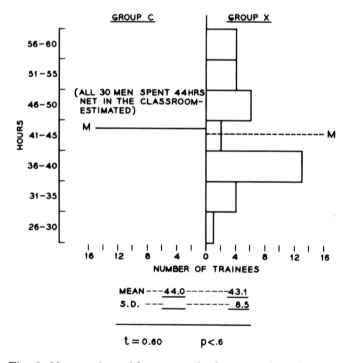

Fig. 8. Net number of hours required to complete the course.

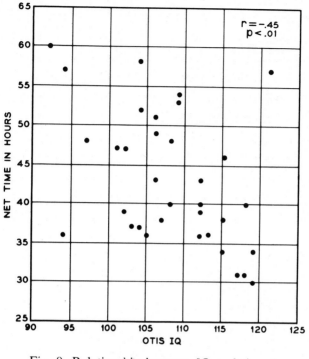

Fig. 9. Relationship between IQ and time for
self-instruction group.

trainees ranging from 30 hours taken by the fastest man to
60 hours taken by the slowest man. An interesting incidental
finding of this study is that there is a relationship between
time to complete the course and IQ. The extent of this
relationship is shown in Fig. 9. ($r = -.45$)

The Davis Reading Test was administered both before
and after training to determine whether or not there would
be an improvement in reading skills in the X group as a
result of reading through the program. The results are

summarized in Fig. 10. The difference between the means is not statistically significant ($P < .2$).

Approximately six months after completion of training, the two proficiency measures, the Facts Examination and the Concepts Examination, were administered again to all men in both groups.[5] A parallel form of the Facts Examination was used and the same Concepts Examination was used. It can be seen in Fig. 11 that the significant differences between the means of the C and X groups which were found immediately after training held up after six months.

Figure 12 shows the comparison of mean scores on the

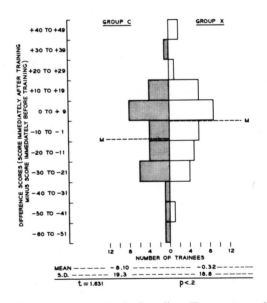

Fig. 10. Changes in Davis Reading Test scores: from pretraining to immediately after training.

5. One man in each group was unavailable for retesting.

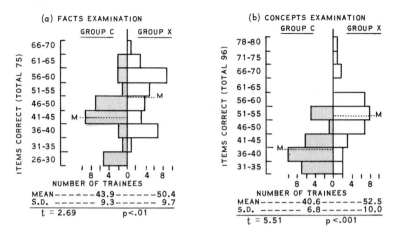

Fig. 11. Distribution of scores on two criterion tests: six months after completion of training.

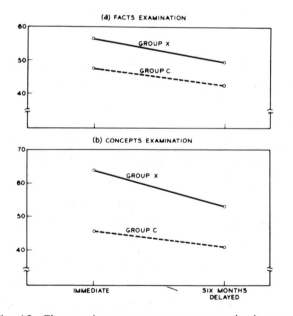

Fig. 12. Changes in mean scores on two criterion tests: immediately after training and six months later.

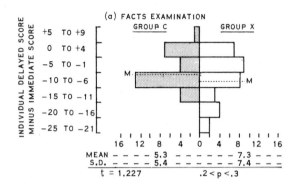

Fig. 13. Six-months post-test. Comparison of difference scores for

two criterion tests immediately after training and six months after training. It is apparent that mean scores dropped after the six-months interval.

It is worthwhile to see if one group dropped significantly more than the other. Figure 13a shows that there was no significant difference between the C and X groups in difference scores on the Facts Examination. On the Concepts Examination, however, a significant difference was found between groups as shown in Fig. 13b. This drop in scores, however, was not sufficiently large to erase the over-all significant difference between groups on the Concepts Examination six months after completion of training. In fact, even though scores tended to drop during the six-months interval,

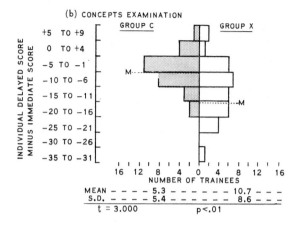

the two treatments; individual delayed score minus immediate score.

mean scores of the X group at the end of that time on both tests were higher than mean scores of the C group immediately after training.

To obtain a measure of the relative effectiveness of the teaching machine and programed book modes of presentation, classes constituting the X group were divided randomly, half the trainees working through the program on teaching machines and half in programed booklets. As shown in Table 2, no significant differences were found between the means of groups on either criterion examination or in the time taken to complete the course. Since these results are in line with those found in the field pilot study, no further analysis of these data was undertaken.

TABLE 2

*Mean Scores on Three Criterion Measures for
Groups Working on Programed Booklets and
Teaching Machines; Immediately after Training*

Criterion Variable	Books N=18	Machines N=16	Significance Levels
Facts Examination	58.0	57.1	$.8 < p < .9$
Concepts Examination	64.1	63.2	$p = .8$
Time to Complete Course	44.6	41.4	$.3 < p < .4$

SUMMARY

A self-instruction program was written to match as closely as possible a basic electricity course offered by a telephone company plant school. Thirty-four telephone company technicians were taught by use of the self-instruction program, and thirty technicians were taught by the conventional lecture-discussion method. The self-instruction (X) group and the lecture-discussion (C) group were found to be approximately equivalent on four control variables.

Both groups were given two criterion tests (the Facts Examination and the Concepts Examination) immediately upon completion of training. Mean scores of the X group on both measures were significantly higher at the .001 level than mean scores of the C group. The significant differences between means held up on retention testing six months after completion of training. Mean classroom time taken to complete the course was approximately the same for both groups, although, due to self-pacing, there was a wide range in the amount of time taken by individuals in the X group.

In addition to the major findings indicated above, two hypotheses about self-instruction were investigated, with the following results: (1) there was no significant improvement in reading skill in the X group, even though the self-instruction program called for much careful reading; and (2) there was no significant difference, either in proficiency or in time, between the achievement of students using teaching machines and those using programed books.

DISCUSSION

DR. ROBERT M. GAGNE: The study that Dr. Holt has reported seems to be a very good one, and perhaps I should say, even an excellent one. It is particularly valuable to have some solid evidence of what a program can accomplish in terms of imparting factual knowledge, of teaching students to apply this knowledge and to retain it over a six-month period. Furthermore, it seems to me of value to know how much time and effort was expended by the learners in going through a learning program, as compared with listening to lectures. Each of these things that we have learned from this paper is needed in making the practical decisions one needs to make in considering whether or not to use a learning program for training, and in determining the particular conditions required for the effective use of such a program. These are, therefore, important and useful findings. They add yet another bit of evidence to the accumulating store which testifies to the effectiveness of learning programs in accomplishing instructional aims.

The study has been done with care, and the evidence it provides is substantial and relatively comprehensive. Therefore, I should like to make some reflections of a general nature concerning the philosophy and implications of this type of study and use Dr. Holt's study to illustrate some points. I think there are some important questions which all of us who are interested in learning programs must face, and it is about these I should like to say something.

The main problem seems to me to be this: How does one assess the effectiveness of a program? I think there are two different ways to answer that question. They are equally important, but in need of distinction. First, the one used in this study is to find an answer to a practical question, will a learning program do the required job of training? Is it as good or better than some currently used method? How does it compare with some method or some absolute value in terms of cost? What is the time required? What is the acceptability of the program? A number of other questions also might be asked about the use of a programed learning technique in practical training situations. Many of these questions were answered in this study by Dr. Holt.

Now, this procedure seems to me to be like an engineering test. It really asked, does the method meet certain criteria, or perhaps even exceed them? There are various program criteria which need to be met, and the question asked by such studies, it seems to me, is the extent to which a program will meet these criteria in bringing about training. As is well known, the answer obtained in this kind of study is a fairly specific one. One is questioning how well this specific program works in this particular situation, with this particular group of people, or with this particular content, under the conditions that obtain here for the lecture situation on the one hand, and the programed learning situation on the other.

Notice that there are limitations on the generality of the conclusions that can be drawn. From such results, we cannot really say a program is better than a lecture, because, of course, that depends on how good the lectures were. Dr. Holt has told us that some home study was involved in one of the groups, but we do not know exactly how much. All of these things tend to limit the generality of this finding. I am not saying this to disparage the study or to down-grade its importance. I think it is a very important one. This study provides the first kind of answer that one can get to this question of the effectiveness of a learning program.

But there is perhaps a more basic answer to the question, how good is programing? This is not an answer for specific purposes, but a general one. If one is going to answer this kind of question, I suggest that comparisons with lectures are quite inappropriate. To answer this more general question, we must have an absolute standard. In fact, what we really must have is a situation in which at least some of the people who are trained by means of a program achieve absolute and perfect mastery of the subject, not just 80%, or one standard deviation above the mean, for example, but absolute mastery. Then we can really begin to ask questions about the artifacts which prevent perfect achievement by everyone, whether they are factors connected with time, errors, basic ability, or whatever.

To repeat, I am simply saying that there seem to me to be two kinds of answers to this question of program effectiveness. The first is a practical answer of the sort represented in this fine study reported by Dr. Holt. The other is the more basic and general answer. For this purpose the comparison of two groups which are given different treatments seems to me to be inappropriate, unless we first solve the problem of establishing an absolute standard of achievement. I therefore think that what is needed most for this general question is to discover how to insure that some people learn everything they are being taught, not just a percentage of it.

McNamara: Thank you very much, Dr. Gagne. We are now ready for a general discussion.

Cook: Dr. Holt, you reported a correlation of —.45 between Otis IQ and the time taken by trainees to complete the programs. Do you have any data on the correlation between the Otis IQ test and the criterion test administered after the trainees completed the program?

Holt: Yes, there is a correlation. I do not recall if it is significant. It is a little lower. The correlation I mentioned was the highest we obtained between two variables.

Cook: Well, that means that the correlation between completion times and final achievement test scores would also be lower. Is that so?

Holt: Yes. Others you might have asked about are the correlations between pre-knowledge of electricity and other factors.

Cook: Did you compare the experimental and control group with respect to those correlations?

HOLT: Yes, there were no differences. They were lower in both instances.

COOK: Well, it is interesting simply to know in which order correlations come out, not their absolute value.

Dr. Gagne, do you know of any course at the college level where achievement is measured in terms of an absolute standard?

GAGNE: I would say, if you want a general answer, that I abhor most educational practices in this area. The notion of measuring achievement on the basis of how students compare with their peers is a useless procedure. Achievement ought to be measured on the basis of what people know, regardless of what somebody else knows. I think this issue has come to the fore because of teaching machines. It seems to me that whatever theory one has about them—and I assure you that mine is not like anyone else's you have ever heard—they are looked upon as a means by which an individual can achieve some specified kind of behavior. Now, that does not mean he does it more or less well. It means that he acquires something new. Now I think what he acquires is, let's say generally, knowledge.

Let's take an example. Suppose you had a little program designed to teach people to add fractions. Let me restrict this to fractions with whole numbers in them. It is not a matter of how well an individual adds fractions, it is a question of can he do it, or can't he? And that's all there is to it. And if he cannot do it, then possibly one would conclude that there was something wrong with the program. You see the tremendously greater control you have over behavior if you look at it this way. I certainly agree with you that there are very few courses in school, or college, or anywhere else that are looked upon this way. I think it is also true that there are altogether too few learning programs which are evaluated in this way. It seems to me that the basic notion of a learning program should be that everybody gets everything right. If they do not, then you ask why.

Question: Does intelligence have an effect on this?

GAGNE: Yes. My own guess would be that the effect of intelligence is to make a difference in the rate with which people learn. This, of course, is consistent with Dr. Holt's results which produced a significant negative correlation ($-.45$) between intelligence level and time required to complete the program.

McNAMARA: You talk about complete mastery. Suppose you used a given method in teaching people how to add fractions and then gave them a 100-item test. If they got all of the answers right, would you say they had a complete mastery of fractions?

GAGNE: Yes.

McNAMARA: Suppose then 20 minutes later you gave them another 100 problems and they got one wrong, then what would you say?

GAGNE: There is of course a question here of measurement error. If you are just talking about one wrong, I think it might be a measurement error.

McNAMARA: Suppose a student had two wrong?

GAGNE: You can presumably devise a technique for calculating the amount of measurement error to be expected, just as one does in the physical sciences. So that you could say that everything was right within the limits of variation in student behavior. For example, suppose there are ten or fifteen wrong. I don't know what this measurement error is, but I suppose that I would begin to be concerned about it intuitively, if it got to be ten wrong out of a hundred.

DEESE: I could not agree more with the notion that some standard of output or performance ought to be the criterion against which any learning program should be evaluated, be it a formal program of this sort or a more conventional course of instruction. But there is one problem which I think is a little different than the accuracy of measurement of the outcome. This is the problem of *when* you should measure performance. Somewhere back in the 7th grade, perhaps, I learned to calculate square roots by the method ordinarily taught in school. I think my performance was pretty close to 100% accurate when I got through. However, I don't think I could do that now without an awful lot of current relearning on my part. So the problem of when to measure performance seems to me very important in evaluating the program, because we know that human retention is extremely fallible and under the influence of a number of conditions of experience. What do you have to say on the subject of retention?

GAGNE: I guess I would say that I would measure more or

less immediately. If you want to ask the question about retention, and I agree with the idea that it is an important question, you are then concerned with forgetting.

DEESE: Let me then ask a question of Dr. Holt. I gather you did not have a correlation between retention loss and time to complete the program. I would expect that your correlations would be unreliable in view of the size of the sample studied.

HOLT: I don't recall.

DEESE: There are theoretical grounds for supposing that program completion time would be directly related to retention loss. The other question is, what did your people do for six months? Were they working on the kinds of jobs for which the program had trained them?

HOLT: I do not think that any other part of the study gave us more trouble than retention testing. We devoted hours to discussion of the question that you have just asked, and to others, such as how to get all of these people back together for testing. In answer to your question, we administered a questionnaire asking what they had done in the intervening six months. I did not mention it before because when we tried to analyze the results, we found that essentially there was no difference that we could put our finger on between men in the two groups in terms of what they had been doing. These people were all switchmen. They were technicians who had moved up a couple of notches in the craft hierarchy, and the general answer is that they went back to their switching jobs.

DEESE: Were they employing during that six month period what they had learned in the program?

HOLT: Our subject matter specialist tried to apply his expert opinion to answering that question. He tried to evaluate what they had been doing and its relation to what they had been taught. Although we found no measurable differences, there was some variation.

However, the question implies something which, as far as I am concerned, is much more important. That is, what was the relevance of this course to their jobs?

DEESE: Right. I think this is particularly relevant to Dr. Gagne's comments. If you are implying an absolute standard by measuring with some formal testing procedure what these people have learned, you also must have some kind of absolute standard by which to evaluate the transfer to various situations, including the situation of working at whatever they are supposed to be learning in the course.

HOLT: One of the difficulties for this particular subject matter is that there is no completely direct job application. The very term "Basic Electricity" implies the type of course it is, namely, a course basic to other courses. In other words, trainees do not go from taking basic electricity into some particular job activity for which this prepares them. They go from this into a course in transmission or something else of that nature.

GLASER: Just to reflect on a couple of the points, especially retention. I think a very significant aspect has been hit upon. I remember a study we did some years ago in which Air Force trainees tested in the World War II pilot program were retested ten or fifteen years later. Some of the tasks were similar to tasks reported in skill and aging studies, where the general trend of the retention curve always shows that there is a loss in skill with age. In contrast, our study showed improvement with age on tasks related to the current life activities of the subjects. The most interesting implication of the study was that if you measure what Holt indicated were life-relevant activities rather than the laboratory tasks measured in the usual aging studies, then you find that skills increase with age. The question about retention or loss of skill, therefore, has to be directed toward developing some criterion that is a function of time and use. At the present time, we do not do this at all well.

Recently, I have come to use the words, norm-referenced measures vs. criterion-referenced measures. Psychological testing has grown up around the idea that a measure is only meaningful if it is based on normative data. You are taught in basic courses on testing that you need to develop a percentile score, a z-score, or some other norm-referenced score, and that a score is only meaningful in relationship to the group for which it is obtained. These are what I call relative or norm-referenced measures. These days, however, with improvement in training techniques, we are being forced more and more to think in terms of achievement, accomplishment or skill as measured by absolutes, or criterion-referenced measures. These measure the behaviors which comprise particular levels of proficiency, without regard to a normative group.

Dr. Gagne's remarks about the kind of research required, that is, finding out why a program has not taught and how it can teach perfectly, suggests the next step following such excellent studies as Dr. Holt's. At the present stage of the game, let us realize that programing is very crude, and we need the results of certain comparative studies. Later, we can follow up with the kind of question which Dr. Gagne brings up so that maybe the next time and the time after that, as we can identify more of the relevant factors involved, we will get closer and closer to attaining and measuring absolute performance.

HUGHES: I would like to get back to the use of absolute standards for evaluating programs. Dr. Gagne mentioned that the next step in research, as Dr. Glaser said, would be the follow-up study using absolute standards of measurement to see if the variables associated with programed instruction could be manipulated to increase or decrease the efficiency of a program. I was wondering whether we could not settle for a fairly stable, reliable standard of measurement rather than an absolute standard. We would then still be able to compare the results obtained from making variations in programs and still be able to say what effect these had on the effectiveness of programed instruction. An absolute standard, after all, is only a theoretically obtainable standard. In actual measurement practice, it is impossible to obtain.

Wouldn't a stable, reliable standard of measurement therefore do just about as well?

GAGNE: What I was suggesting was that although I do not see anything wrong with such studies, I think they yield a limited amount of information. All I was trying to suggest is that you get a tremendously greater amount of information if you can design studies which will show what the factors are in the situation or in the individual which prevent him from achieving the standard of performance we have set for him. Otherwise, you do not have control over these factors. All you know is that one group has reached a certain level of achievement, and another one has either a lower or a higher level. But you are unable to relate the variables in the situation to these differences in as precise a way as I would like to see done in basic research. Now, mind you, I do not think that everybody should do basic research. I think that studies like Dr. Holt's are tremendously valuable and it is important to do them. I don't think that they require this kind of absolute measurement. But when we achieve such measurement, the whole business of evaluating programs, whether it is done in a practical study or not, will have much greater meaning.

GLASER: I would go back to John Hughes' remark regarding a stable as opposed to an absolute measure of performance. Suppose you want someone to do square roots by a particular method. You develop the most efficient program which teaches him that method and permits him to remember it for a while, assuming he uses it. I interpret your concept of stability to mean that after training, your students reach a level of performance which is stable enough so that you can say, this is the level of performance I usually get. But suppose this stable level of performance is not as high as you would like your students to achieve? This method may not force you to revise your training procedures to get where you want to go, that is, to teach the kind of behavior you want to teach.

HUGHES: Suppose your object is to teach square roots. Now, you propose to measure the performance of people to whom you have taught square roots. If you insist on absolute standards, theoretically, this would mean that everyone gets all the square root problems correct and if anyone gets any problems incorrect, then he has not achieved the standard. You, therefore, have a dichotomous measure, either a trainee achieves the standard or he does not. It is not a continuous measure of achievement.

GLASER: It is absolute in the sense that a pilot flying between New York and Pittsburgh either successfully makes the trip or he does not. I think that is a fairly absolute standard. You do not have any of those in education.

HUGHES: But I would imagine that the capability of pilots flying from New York to Pittsburgh differs very significantly. You would be throwing away this difference in ability.

DEESE: Of course, it depends upon what you choose. If you are teaching someone to do square roots, you want to make sure that they do in some sense, achieve some absolute standard. Now suppose you have a statistical assistant and you wish to teach him to do some operation on a calculator. You also want to make sure that he can do it with perfect accuracy. Necessarily forcing the one criterion may allow another criterion to vary, and this is another side to the question of absolute results. You may find that your assistants A and B both performed with 100% accuracy, but A takes twice as long to do the operation. Since you are up against some fundamental individual differences here, are you willing to accept the slower speed as an acceptable criterion performance? It is in multiple tasks which have large numbers of multiple criteria that you get these distributions of achievement. If the distribution occurs with respect to any one measure, it is because you are allowing different criteria levels on other criteria as well.

SEIDEL: Haven't we really opened up a veritable Pandora's box relating to speed now? When you mentioned different criteria or multiple criteria, you must presume that you have some standard of measurement within each of these sub-tasks or sub-criteria. You must also presume that you have a program which will train to a given criterion. If you find certain discrepancies from mastery after teaching with that program, there are two things to look for. One is whether the program is faulty—or the lecture for that matter—or whether we have not specified in sharp enough relief what we want to teach the person.

DEESE: That is possibly the critical question. I gather because there were two major achievement criteria in
Dr. Holt's study, the objective factual test and the concepts test, that in some real sense Dr. Holt was looking
for different criteria. These, however, are pretty *ad hoc*
and intuitive ways of dividing things, and it seems to
me, again from a standpoint of basic research in this
area, we have to have some rigorously stated and logically
consistent notions about what criteria we will employ.
What is it that this factual test is measuring that is
different from the concepts test? And what are we looking for, what do we expect the different programs to
achieve? These are pretty gross and crude criteria that
we have now.

SEIDEL: Yes, even when we go back to the educational field
where at least we can deal with something independent
of the job-relevant material, there are difficulties. We
think we are getting something pure and we are not at
all. We may not want to teach square roots as such, but
perhaps square roots preliminary to using a calculator,
or preliminary to taking other courses where square
roots will be a necessary part. We must consider the
future context in which this material will be used.

O'DONNELL: Dr. Holt, was this done originally—was the
viewpoint of the criteria taken at the time the program
was developed? Or was the initial emphasis on the
content of the existing training course? In other words,
I am asking whether at the time the program was constructed there was emphasis placed on how that content
would be used by trainees in later courses or on the job.

HOLT: I guess one way of answering that question is that we have up until recently successfully resisted the demands from the operating companies of A. T. and T. that this program be published, primarily because we hold no brief for the content. You will recall I said that we tried to match an on-going course. The opinion of those people who have worked on it is that much of the content in this course is not relevant to the job that the craftsmen held. But we simply overlooked that question. It may not be clear to some of you why I insisted on changing the title of this talk. It's an exploratory study. We wanted to wade into programing. That was the main purpose.

Question: What criteria were used in the selection of people to take the program?

HOLT: Well, we had nothing to do with that. It's the kind of situation in which an established training center offers a course, and the people in the field send men to that course who are supposed to be ready to take it and who need it. Practically everybody who came into this particular course was a switchman, so this appears to be one of the criteria.

Question: How does a trainee get to be a switchman?

HOLT: Through an informal selection process. He is probably brought in from what we call an outside plant, where he climbs poles, connects cables, etc. Undoubtedly the people who get to be switchmen are brighter than the men who stay on the poles. But it is all very informal.

Question: Could you add any comments on the experiences

of the trainees with the two methods of programed instruction, the books versus the machines? Your reported
differences there were not of significance. Were there
any other differences reported by interview or questionnaire or observation regarding motivation, appeal, etc.?

HOLT: Well, we have a lot of informal data. For one pilot
group, a small group, we used a balanced experimental
design and switched people from books to one machine
and then to another kind of machine. We asked them
about their preferences. We found no differences in
preference in the pilot study. We found no instances of
people working on books who wanted to change to machines, or vice-versa.

O'DONNELL: I'm curious about one point. I understand that
there was an instructor who stayed with the group that
was working on programed instruction. Did he observe
any flipping back and forth or cheating among the
trainees who used the programed texts?

HOLT: Yes, there was some. At first the men were asked
to use the books as if they were machines. They, of
course, knew they were participating in an experiment,
but some cheating was observed. As we began to see
the evidence coming in from other studies about the
negligible effects of cheating, we began to lose interest
in its importance as far as learning is concerned.

COOK: This discussion is in a way characteristic of discussions of presentations of findings on programing.
What it has done is to raise a large number of fundamental questions. Although these questions have been

with experimental psychologists for a long time, I think
we should read these questions the right way. The fact
that they are being raised is a result of the appearance
of a kind of data which permits them to be taken seriously, I will not say for the first time, but on a far more
extended scale. I think we ought not to get drowned in
them. I don't mean that they are not important—they
are—but you should remember that, instead of saying
that these questions have not been answered, the fact
that they are being raised is a significant social factor.
Something has come along which suggests that these
questions—at least some of them—can be profitably
re-opened. For example, take the question of why the
units of behavior are such that, when we work them out,
we will not be looking at norms any more, but will be
characterizing performance in generic terms, so to speak.
That is a great question. I just want to make sure that
people who have been doing the development work in
the area do not get told that since you have not yet
analyzed the question of what the units of behavior are,
this study ought not to have been done, or the method
ought not to have been experimented with. Something
has been launched which can converge now from a lot
of these questions. I think we may even drop some of
the questions, such as that of measurement error. When
we want to teach somebody how to take square roots,
we want to teach him how to take square roots all the
time with complete accuracy. In fact, this is achieved.
People can do this. All we have to do is to make explicit

II

APPLIED RESEARCH

ON PROGRAMED INSTRUCTION AT THE

EASTMAN KODAK COMPANY *

J . S . B R U C E †

I appreciate the opportunity to make a case presentation at a meeting of this nature. At Kodak we feel the work of the Foundation is valuable and deserves support. In the field of human behavior other people are doing much of the research and we attempt to apply their findings. This is what we at Kodak have done with the work of Professor Skinner. We have applied his programed instruction research to our training programs. This report on how we have applied programing research is divided into two parts: (1) the background on programed instruction at Kodak and (2) an experience with program revision.

* Portions of this chapter were published previously in the *Training Directors Journal,* February 1962. We wish to thank the American Society of Training Directors for permission to reprint them here.
† Director of Training, Eastman Kodak Company.

One of the responsibilities of the Kodak Training Departments is to provide educational opportunities in areas where they do not exist and where they are needed. Kodak started its first apprentice training program in 1915, its first supervisory training course in 1931, its first formal course in photographic science in 1945, mathematical courses such as design of experiments, statistics and matrix algebra in 1956, and many computer training programs in 1958. We have used or are using programed instruction in all of the above areas.

A. Programs

Where have we obtained our programs? Wherever possible we have purchased commercially available programs and used them, for example:

1. *Descriptive Statistics* by Teaching Materials Corp. has been used in its entirety in some areas.
2. Parts of *Statistical Inference* by Teaching Materials Corp. have been used in our regular statistics course.
3. The Doubleday Tutortext electronics course has been used with technical sales representatives.
4. The *English 2600* course has been used in some of our secretarial courses.

Many other programs have been stocked in our library,

such as *Spanish* by Teaching Materials Corp., *Calculus* by Encyclopaedia Britannica Films, and many others. People borrow these programs at their convenience for use either on company time or on their own time. An accurate estimate of the number of people at Kodak using commercial programs is difficult to obtain, but I should guess that about 125 people, in and out of our regular courses, have used all or parts of the commercially available programs.

Some of our programs have been home-grown. These programs, and the number of people who have completed them are as follows:

1. A course in Sensitometry—about 200 people.

2. A course in Maslow's Theory of Human Motivation—about 100 people.

3. Four basic programs in photography—about 275 people.

4. Slide Rule—about 40 people.

5. An Electronic Data Processing System—about 460 people.

As of now about 1,200 people in Kodak have used programed instruction in some form.

The Electronic Data Processing System program was written by Mr. Gurney Weaver of the Roll Coating Division (film support making) at Kodak Park. This 800-frame program is designed to teach functions of a new electronic production data collection and reporting system and a new product identification numbering system. Operators and supervisors learn how to make product data entries on 18 different IBM cards, assign product identification numbers, and perform other duties under the new systems.

In 1962 slightly over four hundred operators and supervisors in the Roll Coating Division were taught this new system by programed instruction followed by discussion. The program consisted of eight parts. As soon as a group of eight to twelve trainees completed a part, they met and discussed the contents of that part. The trainees averaged ten and one-half hours with the programed material and seventeen and one-half hours of discussion. The complete success of this programing approach was demonstrated one week after the system was put into operation with an error level (percentage of cards containing errors) of only one percent.

The same systems change was made in 1961 with a small group of operators and supervisors in one area of the Roll Coating Division. The instruction in this case was by conventional methods: eight two-hour sessions which consisted of lectures, discussion and the use of visual aids such as charts, flow diagrams, and replicas of IBM cards. Four months after the training period, it was found that the error level was 15 percent. Since this error level was definitely too high for efficient operation of the system, four more two-hour lectures and discussions were conducted with the personnel concerned. Within three more months the error level was down to 2-3 percent. A comparison of results by the conventional method and by programed instruction is shown in Figure 1.

The programed material was presented by paper work-

Date	Number of People Involved	Training Methods Used	Time	Error Level
1/61	43	Lectures and discussions with visual aids	16 hours 8 more hours	15% after 4 months 2-3% after 3 more months
5/62	418	Programed instruction and discussion	28 hours	1% after 1 week

Fig. 1. Comparison of results of teaching new electronic production data collection and reporting system by conventional method and by programed instruction.

book and by Kodak-built teaching machines using microfilm. In a survey afterwards, exactly as many people said they preferred the teaching machine as preferred the workbook. The most common observations of those who liked the teaching machine were that they could concentrate better and found the material very easy to understand. Eighty-eight percent of the group said programed instruction, followed by an opportunity for discussion, was the teaching method they liked best for this type material.

All of the foregoing programed material is of the Skinner or Crowder type where the response is verbal. Four skill response programs have been developed for use in assembly line training.

We program parts of a course and make use of those parts as they are finished, rather than waiting for the entire subject. Our approach here can be illustrated in the course

of basic black-and-white photography. This course is normally taught in 12, 4-hour sessions by lecture, lecture-demonstration, laboratory, assigned reading and extensive use of
slides and movies. Figure 2 shows the course content along
with our decisions as to which sections we should try to
program. The checkmarks in the last column indicate those
sections which have been programed.

At this young stage in the development of programed instruction, I think we would have to say that, theoretically,
the entire course content could be programed. However, two

	COURSE CONTENT	TO PROGRAM	COMPLETED
I.	History	NO	
	Basic Camera	YES	✓
	General Photographic Process	YES	✓
II.	Exposure	YES	✓
	Elementary Photographic Optics	YES	
	Elementary Photographic Chemistry	YES	
III.	Film, Manufacturing & Characteristics	YES	✓
IV.	Paper	YES	
V.	Basic Sensitometry	YES	✓
VI.	Contact Printing & Enlarging	NO	
VII.	Laboratory	---	
VIII.	Filters & Lens	NO	
IX.	Exposure Aids - Light Sources	NO	
X.	Photo Products and Uses	NO	
XI.	Laboratory	---	
XII.	Laboratory	---	

Fig. 2. The course content of basic black-and-white photography,
those sections which we decided to try to program,
and those sections which have been programed.

basic questions have to be answered: "Is it economically feasible?" and "Is it educationally wise to do so?" We all know that it is very time-consuming and very expensive to get material programed; therefore, each section of the course was carefully judged as to its importance to the final objectives of the course, its difficulty to the student, its difficulty to the programer, and its subject matter permanency.

As a result of this evaluation, basic camera, general photographic process, exposure, elementary photographic optics, elementary photographic chemistry, film, paper, and basic sensitometry were selected to be programed. These sections are most essential to the final course objectives of teaching the student to use basic B&W photographic terms and principles properly, and to apply these terms and principles to new photographic situations.

History was judged to be relevant material but not essential to the course objectives. For our courses, history is used as an introduction to the course or it is sprinkled throughout the course for enrichment, variety, or change of pace.

With contact printing and enlarging, and filters and lenses, it was felt that the current method of lecture-demonstrations followed by laboratory practice would be hard to improve upon.

The final two sections, exposure aids and light sources, and photo products and their uses, were judged to be too changing in material content to warrant programing.

We look at programed instruction as another excellent teaching method which is at our disposal. When we design a course, we analyze each section to determine, from an educational and economic standpoint, which teaching method best fits the material. We all realized that programed instruction is not the answer to all our training problems, but just another useful teaching tool along with lectures, lecture-demonstrations, laboratory projects, and other methods. The constant use of any one teaching method would soon get tiresome and monotonous; so we feel that the best training programs are those that use several carefully integrated teaching methods.

In summary, our philosophy on programs is that we use commercially available ones wherever possible. In those subject areas where commercial programs either do not exist or do not fit our need, we have our own people write them.

B. *Programers*

What about our experience with programers? At the start, we naively felt that we would get home-grown programs from our regular instructors in addition to their regular teaching assignments. Just teach them how to program and they would do it, or so we thought. With two or three exceptions, this effort has been an outstanding failure. Some individuals, notably James Sucy and Arthur Fraser of the Kodak Park Training Department, did write successful programs in addition to their regular teaching load. These individuals were intrigued by the process of programed instruction and constructed programs as parts of courses they were currently teaching. I might add that in spite of their success, these two individuals have only written one program apiece. Each program is approximately 150 frames.

When it became apparent that the construction of programs was going to be a full-time job, we had a two-way choice: (1) assign a regular instructor to writing programs, or (2) take a subject specialist, teach him how to program, and assign him full time to constructing programs. We chose the latter course and picked Richard Knight, an engineering physicist, graduate of the University of Maine, and for seven years a product specialist in the Film Testing Division.

What criteria did we use to select Knight? We liked the way he reacted to the challenge. We liked his record in Film Testing. Above all, we liked the fact that he wanted to program. We were very fortunate. Knight has turned out to be a good programer. (Incidentally, the three programers I have mentioned, Fraser, Sucy, and Knight, are from the State of Maine. I don't know whether this is significant or just coincidental, but you may at least consider it an interesting sidelight.)

We do not yet have any good statistical evidence as to what kind of people are the best teaching machine programers. However, in the electronic data processing field, we do have statistical evidence on over 100 individuals to show what kind of people make the best computer programers. Let me emphasize that programing for teaching machines and programing for computers are two completely different types of programing. However, many people feel that both fields of programing require individuals who have similar personality traits.

At Kodak, computer programers are given a test battery consisting of (1) International Business Machine Programmer Aptitude Test, (2) Brown-Carlson Listening Comprehension Test, and (3) the Edwards Personal Preference Schedule. Dr. Charles Upshall, a Kodak psychologist, tells me that the correlation is very high between the results of this battery and the proficiency on the job of writing programs for the computer. As yet we do not have a large enough sample of people who have written teaching machine programs to compare the results of their scores on this test battery. Knight has taken the above test battery and the psychologists would recommend him highly for a computer programing job. Dr. Upshall said to me, "Any conclusions you jump at from that scant bit of data are yours and yours alone."

C. Student Reaction

What has been student reaction to programed instruction? This is a full subject in itself. I think we can make two generalizations: (1) everywhere we have used it the reaction has been, on the whole, favorable. During a recent application we had one person complain because he had not been taught this way before, (2) the negative responses have come from people whose skill or knowledge is beyond what we are trying to teach. These people may feel that it is too elementary or too slow. You might expect this reaction from any individual who is proficient and is put into a beginning learner's group.

D. Control Groups

What about control group studies? We have two experiences: (1) The Maslow Theory of Human Motivation constructed by Fraser and (2) the sensitometry program by Sucy. In the motivation session a control study was made of the recall of 60 key words of the Maslow theory. One group took this course in programed form; another group of 38 people received the same material by lecture. On a recall six weeks after the presentation of the material, the control group recalled 13.5 percent and the programed group recalled 26.8 percent (Figure 3).

	LECTURE APPROACH	PROGRAMMED APPROACH
3. Please diagram as much of this theory as you can recall. (The material that finally appeared on the blackboard.)		
MASLOW - AIR FORCE THEORY OF HUMAN MOTIVATION	13.5	26.8

Fig. 3. Percent recall of 60 key words of the Maslow
Theory six weeks after the course.

Another control group study was made of Sucy's sensitometry program. Sensitometry is a mathematical and graphical means of defining the speed and quality characteristics of photographic emulsions. It is a method used extensively in all of our quality control departments, and one of the very important subjects taught in all of our technical photographic courses. Two groups of ten people each were used as a lecture control and compared to three groups of ten people each who took the material by programed instruction. As a pretest Sucy gave all five of his groups 16 multiple-choice questions on sensitometry sprinkled through a 40-question test on photography. This pretesting is a standard procedure to determine how much photographic knowledge the production staff people have before they are sent to this course. At the end of the course he used the same 16 questions sprinkled through a group of 56 questions. The results were as follows:

	Pre-Test	Post-Test	Difference
Control Group	40%	84%	44%
Programed Group	38%	87%	49%

Statistically we can say that this is in the right direction but the difference is not significant. This program on sensitometry has been used with about 200 people, but after the first study no more control groups were run. It was apparent that the programed material did as good a job as the lecture in explaining the material, and the use of this program cut the instructor's time with the students from two hours to one-half hour. Another benefit from programing which we sometimes overlook is that Sucy and other instructors who have written programs are probably much better teachers because of this experience.

The accuracy of control group studies is dependent to such a large extent on the quality of the control teaching technique and on the quality of the program that this became a rather time consuming endeavor and one of dubious worth. Thus, rather than run more control studies, we prefer to spend our energy analyzing a program and revising it to accomplish our objectives.

PROGRAM REVISION

So much for background, now let's look in more detail at our experience with one course.

I have mentioned Knight's first efforts with the basic camera and the exposure programs, both of which were parts of a larger program. When he finished this material he used it in a secretarial photographic course.

The program was administered using a flipbook and answer pad. (Figure 4). Each secretary, when she had a break in her daily routine, would be given the course by her supervisor at her regular place of work. The average completion time for the program was about one hour, so that it could be scheduled. The step chart in Figure 5 shows the variation in time required to complete the program. Note that although the mean is about 60 minutes, the range is from 20 minutes to over 120 minutes.

Fig. 4. A secretary using a program in flipbook
and answer pad form.

A similar step chart (Figure 6) was made of the errors
on the program. On the average we achieved a 5 percent
error rate with a range of 0-23 errors.

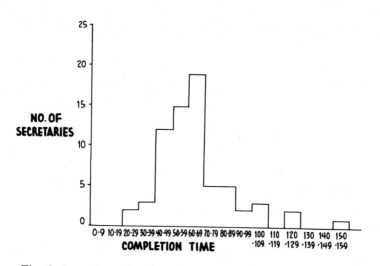

Fig. 5. Step chart showing the variation in time required by 69 secretaries to complete a programed unit in photography.

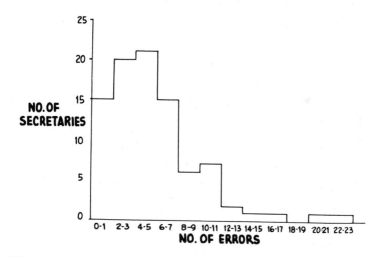

Fig. 6. Step chart showing the variation in the number of errors made by 90 secretaries while doing a 115 frame programed unit in photography.

About two days after the secretaries had completed the 115 frames each was given a quiz covering the material.

We have determined the coefficients of correlation between the following factors:

1) the time of completion and errors in the program—not significant;

2) the test score and the time of completion—not significant;

3) number of errors in the program and the test score—not significant.

Since all of these items showed that we were not getting any significant differences, we decided to make an analysis of the items in the program which resulted in errors on the test.

This analysis illuminated areas of weakness in the program. In a way this is a variation of the old saw that "if the student doesn't learn, the teacher doesn't teach." Our attitude is that if a significant percentage of the students are unable to answer some of the post-test questions which are basic to our teaching objectives, then the program has failed. This is obviously one of the strengths of programed instruction, because it enables you to go directly to the part of your program dealing with that objective, and to make the corrections.

Let's look at a few examples. One of the objectives of the course was to have the learner name the basic parts of the camera and explain the functions of each. When they had finished the 115-frame program, 94% of the people could name the basic parts of the camera, but only 77% knew the functions. (Figure 7).

What has been done in this regard? Let us take for example those frames which dealt with the function of the lens. In the first edition of the program there were only 3 frames (number 24, 28, and 96). In the second edition this has been expanded. With some editorial changes frame 24 of the first program is identical with frame 52 of the second. Frame 28 is identical with frame 86 and frame

INTRODUCTION TO PHOTOGRAPHY		
	MEAN	RANGE
NAME PARTS OF CAMERA	94%	86%-100%
DESCRIBE FUNCTION	77%	43%-100%

Fig. 7. Mean scores and range of scores obtained by the secretaries who completed the "Introduction to Photography" program.

98 is the same as frame 130. But from Figure 8 you will note five added frames for emphasis and drill (numbers 53, 54, 55, 87, and 108).

However, revising a program is not just adding frames. Even more important than adding is rewording the frames for maximum clarity or impact. Let us look at the two following examples. Frame I-17 in Figure 9 contains too

```
                            REVISION

                      Frames Re:  Lens


                 1st Edition            2nd Edition
        Frame         24                    52

                                            53

                                            54

                                            55

                       28                   86

                                            87

                                           108

                       98                  130
```

Fig. 8. Increase from the first edition to the second edition
in number of frames dealing with the function of a lens.

much information. It is confusing because we have intro-
duced two new facts. The revised frame I-17R is more
straightforward, since it is limited to just one new fact.

In frame I-14 of Figure 10 there is a chance of obtaining
a response you do not want. The student can either correctly answer *film* or *light*—two quite different responses but
both correct. Some of the people did this; therefore, the frame
was revised to I-14R. Of the 115 frames in the original
program only 15 frames were unchanged.

Examining another area of difficulty we find a problem
with the concept of the Exposure Value System. By way of
background, exposure (the amount of light hitting the film)

I-17.   A camera is a <u>light-tight</u> <u>box</u> except
for a small hole, aperture, or opening through
which the image of an <u>object</u> (person, place, or
thing) is recorded on a film or _____
-sensitive surface.

I-17R.   A camera is essentially a <u>light-tight</u>
<u>box</u> except for a small hole, opening or aperture
through which _____ is allowed to enter.

Fig. 9. An original frame (I-17) in the first edition of
"Introduction to Photography" and its revised
version (I-17R) in the second edition.

I-14.   When you wish to take a photograph,
a camera is of no value unless you also
have some _____

I-14R.   When you wish to take a photograph,
a camera is of no value unless you also
have some _____ loaded in the camera.

Fig. 10. An original frame (I-14) in the first edition of
"Introduction to Photography," and its revised
version (I-14R) in the second edition.

is controlled in practically all cameras by, (1) the lens opening and, (2) the shutter speed. In many modern cameras
the lens opening and shutter speed are coupled together so
the user, instead of setting them independently, sets what is
called an Exposure Value or EV Number. (Figure 11).

Setting the EV Number then controls the amount of
light reaching the film. An example of this: If you choose an
EV Number of 12, you can double the exposure by going
to an EV Number of 11, or you can halve the exposure by
going to an EV Number of 13. There is an inverse relation-

Fig. 11. Close-up of the lens mount of a camera showing the
Exposure Value Numbers used to control camera exposure.

ship: the lower the number, the greater the exposure. Each number represents two times the exposure of the next larger number. The information I have just given you was the same as the information in the program. Now, before reading the next paragraph, try to answer the following parts of quiz question number 12.

```
12.  Starting with EV-14:
     a.  What EV number represents twice the exposure?
     b.  What EV number represents one-half the exposure?
     c.  What EV number represents one-eighth the exposure?
     d.  What EV number represents four times the exposure?
```

In my explanation of the Exposure Value System, I gave you an example of 12A and 12B; however, you must extrapolate your knowledge to answer 12C and 12D. The correct answers are as follows:

```
12.  Starting with EV-14:
     a.  What EV number represents twice the exposure?        13
     b.  What EV number represents one-half the exposure?     15
     c.  What EV number represents one-eighth the exposure?   17
     d.  What EV number represents four times the exposure?   12
```

Now let's look at the way some 90 secretaries answered this question: 67 percent were right on 12A, 58 percent on 12B but only 33 percent on 12C and D. It is obvious that this concept of the EV System had not been taught to the extent we would have hoped.

At first, we thought that it might be due to lack of ability to handle the arithmetic involved. However, when we went back to the clerical aptitude tests which all of these girls had taken when they joined the company, there was no significant correlation between their arithmetical ability and the way they answered this question. Therefore, the trouble

INTRODUCTION TO PHOTOGRAPHY

Objective		First Edition		Second Edition
		Number of Frames	Test Score	Number of Frames
Define photographic terms		28	60%	65
Name the parts and explain function		26	N-94% F-77%	46
Variables that control camera exposure		19	79%	27
Describe and use:	the traditional method of expressing camera exposure	20	78%	38
	the exposure-value system of expressing camera exposure	14	65%	24
	a table of equivalent exposures	8	92%	10
	TOTAL	115		210

Fig. 12. Analysis of "Introduction to Photography" showing number of frames, test score mean on each objective of the first edition and the greater number of frames in the second edition which were added to try to offset low test scores.

must be that this concept was not illustrated with a sufficient number and variety of examples. We all know that a concept or generalization can only be learned through many, varied, interlocking specifics.

Based on our analysis of similar items, a revision has been made of the program. (Figure 12).

This is a progress report and not a finished report on the subject. Only a few people so far have taken the second edition in rough form. So we shall have to wait until some future time to see how effective these changes have been. People are still using the first edition, since even without changes it is better than anything they have.

What is our feeling on programed instruction at this stage of our experience? It definitely performs a valuable teaching task, and has whenever we have used it. Any dynamic teaching method requires revision, as the instructor checks the final results with the objectives originally set for his course. Programed instruction simplifies this task since frames in a programed course deal with specific objectives. If the final performance results show that these objectives have not been met, then it is fairly simple to go back and revise the frames dealing with these objectives.

DISCUSSION

Dr. Robert Glaser: Jim Bruce has brought up some especially interesting points. There are two main ones and then some subsidiary ones on which I would like to comment. The first main point concerns using control groups or revising programs to obtain a behavioral difference. The other is about concepts.

As a researcher, I think I do some of the same things that Jim has done, only I do one thing more. I think that Jim has hit upon an important notion of programing. That is in manipulating, or trying to arrange learning conditions so that they make a difference in the behavior that you are trying to produce. That is really your main task. You make some manipulations on the basis of past knowledge and past ideas and you actually try to arrange a learning environment so it makes a difference in the behavior of your students. I think that this is what many people attempt to do in the laboratory—make manipulations that lead to a difference in behavior. It is an important endeavor, and I think that programing has emphasized more than ever before that we want our manipulations to make behavioral changes. The payoff for Jim is whether or not he attains his objectives, and so it is not very useful for him to set up control groups.

Now, I do the same thing in the laboratory, but I do one more thing. This is that when I manipulate conditions, I attempt to talk about or describe the conditions I manipulate. This description might be called the learning theory, or the model, or the super-structure which helps me tie together a lot of the things I know about learning. I do not think I do anything different than Jim Bruce does to cause changes in behavior, but I talk about them in terms of some sort of a theoretical framework which helps me to integrate the things I do. The other point is that I probably do not, or should not, go ahead and use control and experimental groups until I can identify a dimension along which my control and experimental groups lie. This is the problem. Suppose you have a conventionally taught group and a programed group, and you do an experiment. The problem is that the operations you perform in conventional teaching and in the program must fall along the same identifiable dimension if you are to discover differences between them. So I guess, as a laboratory researcher, I attempt to identify a dimension, and then I can do a controlled study along that dimension. If I have not identified this dimension, however, a control group study is not very useful.

A second point is that making revisions in programs becomes a very practical matter. You make revisions so that you can produce a particular behavior. As a psychological researcher, my objective in making revisions is to attempt to identify the nature of the revisions in precise terms. Suppose, for example, I write a program, make the revisions, and then identify, in my learning theory terminology, the functions of each of the frames so that I can identify the psychological and pedagogical functions of each frame, and describe my manipulations in some consistent terminology. I would say that I was then getting close to being able to describe, in a consistent set of scientific terms, how I have changed the manipulated behavior.

The point I am making is that I think I am doing things similar to the ones you do to try to change behavior. We both have problems in behavioral manipulation, but perhaps I do one more thing. That is, I try to make contact with a structure so I can tie all the pieces together into some sort of consistent theory, which has other benefits. So I think your concern about the control group studies and about the necessity for making practical changes is groundless. The fact that you say that control groups are not very useful for us at this stage of the game is a perfectly reasonable conclusion, one that other people also have reached. I do not know if I have made the point, but I think that programed instruction brings about this kind of thinking. You have been led directly to it, and I think that is very good.

The other point concerns concept learning. It is a difficult one, because how people learn concepts has been a consistent problem. What do we mean when we teach a concept? Do we want students to be able to apply the concept to a lot of different situations? Do we want them to use it to make a model of the situation? What I am trying to say is that rather than teach a definition and then see whether people can apply it, my tendency is to give them practice in applying the concept. If we want them to learn to apply knowledge to new situations, then a program should provide practice in applying knowledge to new situations. If we want them to build a model of what they know, they should have some practice in building such models. You must identify what you want them to do, and then give them practice in doing it.

The question also arises about students going beyond the practice so they can do new things and use concepts in an ingenious way. The hope is that if we give them the appropriate kind of practice, and this we need to discover, they will be able to generalize beyond the practice we have given them. Too often in teaching a concept we wonder whether they will be able to transfer it or use it.

I am interested in why Jim Bruce's sensitometry program was more effective than his theory of motivation program. His trainees in the former did better in terms of percent of items right on the test. I would make the point that different subject matter structures may require different programing techniques. Imposing one kind of programing on all subject matters will, therefore, probably not be the eventual thing to occur. Different kinds of subject matter, subject matter structure, and subject matter layout will probably require different kinds of programing. If you had used a different kind of programing for the theory of motivation program, you might have obtained results comparable with those obtained with the sensitometry program.

The fact that you obtained no relationship between time to go through the program and achievement test scores suggests that some sort of pacing procedure might be tried. I think that pacing sometimes gets people to work faster. Under the pressure of a deadline, we work much faster and often accomplish the same results in less time than if we did not have a deadline and dawdled along. It seems to me that pacing, that is, making people go through a program at a fixed rate, can be a very efficient procedure.

The finding of no significant correlations between aptitude and achievement test scores is, of course, partly a function of the reduced variability in achievement test results. This points out to me something that I guess will show up increasingly in programing. One gets into more and more trouble in the selection testing end of the business as a result of using programed learning. The correlations between selection tests and final end-of-course achievement test will result in lower validities for the selection tests. This is true because the variability of achievement test scores will be smaller. As you know, the variability of the achievement scores affects the size of the correlation coefficient, so your test validities will be smaller, and you should expect this.

SEIDEL: The exposure example that Jim Bruce used was excellent. It provides a wonderful example of two points.

The first is the one that Bob Glaser spoke of, namely, the function of the revision. You should know what you are revising. The second is something we spoke of before, and that is the apparent relationship between the task criterion and the program itself. One thing I would suggest is to change the numbering system that you have for exposure values so that there is a direct positive retionship between the exposure and the numbering system. There are two things. I can see changing the criteria rather than the program. But I think it points up quite clearly, again in relation to what Bob has mentioned, that you should really know the revision and know the function of the items that you are talking about. Not once in the program was it clearly stated that there is an inverse relationship between the numbering system and the actual exposure condition, that is, the amount of light.

BRUCE: That is stated in the program, though, as I mentioned earlier.

SEIDEL: I remember that Jim Bruce stated that, and I was concentrating on this inverse relationship, but I was thinking about this as an object lesson of what we were talking about before, and I got the last two wrong.

DEESE: I would like to comment on that example, too. In your revised program, what did you emphasize, teaching arithmetic?

KNIGHT: No, I did not teach arithmetic. It was not based on arithmetic. I was simply presenting the rule that in the exposure value system there is an inverse relationship.

I then gave them examples where they doubled and halved what they were given, and they practiced doubling and halving. They did not have practice in going any further, and this was one of the things we threw in to see if they could. In the revision, I am not giving them arithmetic in a sense. I am giving them further practice on what happens when they try to extrapolate, by taking a half or by doubling. If you continue this process, true, it does come down to arithmetic, since a half times a half is a fourth.

BRUCE: This is what Bob Glaser is pointing out. If you are going to teach a concept, then maybe you have to give them practice in the concept.

DEESE: I was going to take a different tack on this. I did not think there was any evidence that you failed to teach the concept. There is another skill involved in the concept, however, which they just did not have. This skill was how to multiply properly to get these numbers. They had the basic idea all right, that it was essentially a logarithmic scale against a linear scale. The sort of thing that Bob Glaser objected to was the nature of the concept itself. Maybe you ought to change your exposure value system. They may well have gotten the concept, but you would not know that, because if a concept involves a set of skills (in this case, arithmetic), which are not readily available to the individual using a program of this sort, he cannot demonstrate to you that he has learned the concept. In order to do this, he must use certain skills that he has difficulty in producing. Then you never know if he knows the concept or not.

The second question concerns your real aim in teaching this part of the program. I presume that the ultimate outcome of such a program is to learn to use a camera. Do you need to put in a step of this sort? In other words, all the trainee needs to know is that there is a linear scale which is inversely related to the amount of light available to him, and how to use the instrument. And I wonder if it is generally true that programs may be unnecessarily lengthened in order to teach a particular eventual outcome which is not needed by the student.

BRUCE: Well, the trainee has to know, when he has half the amount of light available, how to set the camera to compensate for this so he will get the same exposure.

DEESE: But all he need know is how to read from an exposure meter to the exposure value system. Correct?

BRUCE: No. I can measure the amount of light with the exposure meter here, and I know that this is double the amount of light that I would have if the lights were turned out. How would I adjust my exposure? I am measuring the amount of light in the room and I have to know how to adjust the camera to compensate for this.

SEIDEL: This is an interesting point. You should utilize the skills and knowledge that the individual has available when he begins this program, or at the time he is faced with using a camera, let's say. We have all learned in the past that large things have bigger numbers associated with them. More light—bigger numbers. A simple thing like that, I am sure, interferes with the individual trying to sit down and memorize this inverse relationship. Things like this, I think, are important when you consider the transfer value of a program.

McNAMARA: I was wondering if we could get the discussion over to another point which intrigued me a bit. This was covered in the previous presentation and in Bob Glaser's comments about not being concerned with control groups. Does anybody want to speak to that point? Does everybody agree?

Comment: I have a question on that point. It was mentioned that if your control group does either less well or better than your experimental group, you still have the variable of how good an instructor you had with the control group. You also have the variable relating to how good the program was. In doing research, however, if the researcher does not use a control group, is he not then making the assumption that because programed learning is effective in some areas, it is perhaps adaptable to, and the best method for teaching any subject? It would seem that we have no way of testing that assumption unless we do have a control group.

BRUCE: Let's take the situation in which we have 500 IBM punch card operators to train. Now, we could train them by the conventional method, such as flip charts and lecture, and we could train them also by programed instruction. We could set up a control group and train 250 one way and 250 the other way. Then I, or somebody else would have something to report to meetings like this ad infinitum. What we are really interested in, though, is that at the end of this training task the trainees are able to do a job in a certain way. And that is all we are interested in. We have to make sure they can fill out, handle, and have everything in the correct spot on the IBM card at the right time. Our analysis indicated that we could do this best by programed instruction.

MCNAMARA: But don't you have a problem here? Suppose you are now teaching Subject A by some specific method. If you want to teach this subject by programed instruction, you are going to have some time and expense involved in changing over to programed instruction. If you are teaching the subject satisfactorily now, and change over and teach it satisfactorily by programed instruction, you have not gained anything. In addition, it has cost you time and money to make the change. Therefore, it seems to me that you need some comparison. Although you can do it satisfactorily by programed instruction, what is the advantage of doing it this way rather than by whatever other way you have been using, such as telling students to take a book home and read something? It seems to me that you need something to judge against, don't you?

BRUCE: Well, here the question of teacher time becomes important—or staff time spent in preparation of a program versus staff time spent in class. If I can decrease this, I have something in which management is interested. So, the real thing I am interested in is the ability of the learner to perform the task at the end of the learning experience. That is really the main thing I am after.

MCNAMARA: Yes, but if it cost you $50,000 to prepare

the program, you are going to have to save an awful
lot of hours of instructor time to pay for this, aren't
you? If it cost you $5,000 to prepare the program, you
would not have to save very much instructor time.

BRUCE: Well, let's suppose I am currently teaching by
Method A, and I switch over and teach it by programed
instruction. I run control groups and show that programed instruction is now teaching the subject in half
the time, or twice as fast. So I say, "All right, this shows
that programed instruction is fine." Anybody looking
at this figure says, "Well, what was wrong with your
old teaching method?" The question then arises whether
I can improve my old teaching method so that it would
be as effective as programed instruction. As we got into
programed instruction, therefore, we often found ourselves rewriting the lecture.

MCNAMARA: My comment is this. You are teaching course
A at present. You program this and teach it by programed instruction. If your trainees go through the program in half the time, and learn twice as well, you would
say, all right, here is course B which is similar to A, I had
better program that. But if you program course A and
teach it in about the same amount of time with a very
slight gain in learning achievement, and it cost you
considerable money and time to do this, then if you
look at course B, which is similar to it, I believe you
would hesitate before going ahead and programing
course B.

COOK: This discussion is hinging on data generated by relatively short courses, as I understand it. Isn't that so? What was the longest one?

KNIGHT: These courses averaged around an hour to an hour and a half. Of course, you had a span of learning rate or program completion times. The time varied from one half hour to four hours for different persons to go through one of these programs.

COOK: This is an important consideration in thinking of costs and also in looking for effects. I think you can accept it as a general notion that the shorter the course you are programing, the less powerful will be whatever contrasts you are looking for. This also affects the points that Bob Glaser made about the absence of correlations. I think that is a very important point, and a very exciting one, but I would hate to have it hinge solely on data generated by these brief courses.

DEESE: Well, there is a general question about these comparisons. After all, there is a literature now that is some 40 years old on comparisons of teaching methods for different types of subject matter. A number of people have looked at this literature, and the most general conclusion that can be drawn is that method does not make the slightest bit of difference. The differences between Method A and Method B, in any particular subject mater, generally turn out to be very small and marginal differences, whether this is material taught in a couple of hours or over an entire semester. Now, to be sure, these are comparisons between traditional school methods of teaching subjects. There is a great amount of literature, for example, on teaching subtraction. There are two methods of teaching subtraction in public schools, and there are small marginal differences in favor of one or the other method. But the conclusion that you can draw out of these studies, it seems to me, relates to what Jim Bruce has said, namely, that our traditional methods of instruction have already been subjected to improvement—albeit unprogramed, intuitive, haphazard improvement—from time to time so that any further improvement we get is generally going to be small and marginal.

If you do find a big difference between two methods —the program method and the lecture method—then you are presented with the opportunity of going back to the lecture method and seeing what is wrong with the lecture, seeing if you can get it back up to the point where there is not a big difference. The great advantage of programing, it seems to me, is the ease with which one can do revisions of what is being taught, and the analytic power it gives you. You can pull one part out and say this is where the trouble is, as Jim Bruce did. Looking for over-all comparisons seems to me the wrong way to look at it. You should look for the analytic power that a program gives you. Perhaps it is worth the money to provide you initially with a stable point from which you can depart to make these improvements as time goes on and technology increases. Now, when you want to change what you have taught, it can be done in a rational and analytic way.

COOK: If your remarks are prophetic, and I think they are, the question will not be controls versus no controls, but simply the most adequate kind of comparison that can be made with the last version of a program. If you then had a technological framework in which these results could accumulate, feed back, and converge, this would be very productive. This is not even a theory of programing. It is simply a system which allows this to happen.

HOLT: Since we are really talking about management decision factors here, let me add two more to what Jim Deese has just said. These are factors in which we are very much interested. We have a very large volume of training in certain subjects; as a matter of fact, our craft training bill runs up high into eight figures annually. One factor is the reduction in the number of instructors. All of our instructors reported that they did not have enough to do. They were bored. They could have handled three times as many people under the self-instruction set up. The other factor, which I think was implied in what Jim Deese said, is control of the tremendous variation among instructors. We can talk about improving the lecture, but we are really only talking about improving it with one instructor. We have probably 100 people teaching basic electricity in the Bell system, and the variation in excellence of these people is considerable. If you have a program, of course, it always comes out the same way.

CHILDS: Dr. Holt, do you mean that your instructors could

handle three times as many people who have read the program?

HOLT: No, no—if the trainees are working on programs. Our classes are typically ten; in fact, if you divide four into the number in our study, you get less than ten. However, all of the instructors, and we had five who participated in this, said they could easily handle thirty in the self-instruction situation. Furthermore, they do not all have to be studying the same subject matter. As long as the instructor is knowledgeable in whatever the subject matter is, he is able to tutor a man whether he is taking basic electricity, advanced electronics, or transmission.

PETER: It seems to me that Walt McNamara has a point, though, in regard to the management decision factor. It is possible that management may want to allocate some portion of the cost of new programing to research, or development of analytical tools which, in fact, add a great deal of power to general teaching methodology. This may have to be a deliberate allocation of funds to what might be termed a research effort for improving teaching. They also, I should think, want to know the cost per pupil to get him to a certain degree of competence in a particular field, as well as the extent to which programed learning courses, at any stage in time, are equivalent in cost, or more or less expensive than conventional courses. It seems to me that this involves several kinds of economic analyses. Among other things, it would be the distribution of the cost—let's call it a capital cost—for developing the program for the expected number of pupils over a period of time. You could then write off the initial investment for programing over your expected student population. Savings in instructor time would be another thing to be considered. Space savings might be still another, and so on.

There must be a half dozen or so rather easily quantifiable economic factors which would give you a fairly objective determination of the relative cost of a program versus another teaching method, when both are compared with respect to some standard of achievement. This is something that management might be interested in, even though it does not necessarily have any strong theoretical content for the purposes of our present discussion.

GLASER: I have come to call this base-line data. Some other people call it parametric data. It seems to me that rather than thinking of control and experimental groups, you should think in terms of needing base-line data from which you can talk. For instance, we asked how programed learning affects retention. Then we look back to see what we know about retention with conventional teaching methods, and we find nothing that we can call base-line data. We ask questions about these factors Hollis Peter brings up that can be quantified, and it really forces us to look for base-line data so that we know where we started from and can thus measure whether our manipulations make a difference. Therefore, I consider the problem one of providing base-line

data. Maybe that is what you get from your control
group.

Peter: This is a good point, Bob. I was thinking of it when
Ollie Holt was talking about the higher retention level
of the programed learning group six months later. How
much is that increased level of retention worth to management? How much are they willing to invest to get
that higher level in students both at the beginning and
after six months? I don't know that there is any way to
calculate this now, but this requires a base-line type
of calculation, doesn't it?

Holt: Of course, management does not have adequate data
on retention in regard to current teaching methods.

McNamara: Bob, how do you get this base-line data that
you speak of?

Glaser: I suppose I would have to find out something such
as how much do people learn now, or how much have
they learned in the past? I guess I would have to go
out and get either achievement measures or survey
data. I could then say that this is what people achieve
now, this is how much they remember, or this is how
much they can learn in an hour. Maybe then I would
have the data I need to proceed with my revision-type
experiment.

McNamara: I was interested in Jim Bruce's comments
about the portions of the course that he decided to program and the portions that he decided not to program.
How do we determine this? Do we have any data on
which parts we should just forget until four years from

now, or do we have some way of choosing the optimal sequence for attacking a rather lengthy program? Maybe you could elaborate a little bit more, Jim, on how you selected some topics for programing and left others out.

BRUCE: Well, let's take history, for example. History is something that is relevant to the course, but it is not really basic to our objective.

McNAMARA: Isn't history pretty factual, the sort of thing we ordinarily start out with? Isn't this the easiest and most appropriate thing to program? Because it is not necessary to have an interpretation by a lecturer or discussion leader, you can write history in factual terms and very easily put it into a program.

BRUCE: I think, however, that is the wrong reason. The fact that a particular part of the course may be easy to program, I think, is a poor reason to choose that to program.

McNAMARA: Why did you not program it?

BRUCE: Because, again, you have to list the basic objectives of the over-all course. You see, our process was to go back and say, what are the basic objectives of taking this course?

McNAMARA: Why don't you drop the history out? Not teach it at all?

BRUCE: That is a very good question. This is one thing that comes out when you subject a current course to this kind of analysis. Is this part really necessary?

HOLT: Let me suggest a reason why it is there. Vocational training in general, is strongly influenced by the older

Herbartian steps in teaching. These have been brought up-to-date a couple of times, the latest one being during World War II in the JIT (Job Instruction Training) program. I think your history is a residue of step one, which is preparing the student to learn, or getting him interested in the subject and motivated. It is really not included in the course objectives.

GLASER: Let me make a point related to that. Let us say that history is straight factual material. In contrast, I think that the easiest thing to program, based on present notions of verbal behavior, is a principle or rule and the examples in which this rule is used. It is easy to manipulate a generalization by using it in different examples and contexts. That is how most programs seem to do it best. I think it is much harder to program straight facts for retention. We know much less about that.

Secondly, it is also harder to program non-verbal material. I notice that Larry O'Donnell is going to talk later about non-verbal learning, and I will be very interested to hear what he says. The point is, however, that the decision to program seems to lie along these lines. You program the things for which you can make a rule and give examples. To my way of thinking, it is harder to program facts or non-verbal things.

KNIGHT: Let me say a couple of words on the history aspect. It is not completely essential to the course objective. In programs that we have written, however, we have tried to bring in a little bit of it, although we have not hit it as hard as we did in the lectures. I have a feeling that it has value as enrichment, and also, as a change of pace. A program of hard, cold facts all the way through can get somewhat monotonous. So we try to throw in a little bit of history, not as one big chunk at the beginning, but scattered throughout the course, whenever it is appropriate. It gives the student a little extra information, or enrichment, for which he may not be held responsible, and it results in a change of pace which livens up the program.

MCNAMARA: In other words, you did include some history in the programs, then?

KNIGHT: We have thrown in a little bit, a smattering here and there where we thought it was appropriate.

SEIDEL: Along this same line, HumRRO has been responsible for a lot of training innovations in the Army. One thing they came up with was a notion that they call functional context. This relates to a kind of program similar to the one that you are describing and that is implied when Bob Glaser mentions that fact-retention learning is very difficult. The easiest way, and I think the most appropriate way, to teach nomenclature to an individual—and this is what HumRRO did—is to present the nomenclature in the context in which the individual will actually work with it. You do not get him to memorize a whole set of names independent of the acts which he will perform using these particular names. You will find that this is a much better way to teach.

KNIGHT: Let's backtrack a bit. We were talking about the ability our students had to extrapolate, to go from doubling and halving to further aspects of exposure time, and the relationship of this to their ability to handle fractions. This relationship did not show up in our analysis of I.Q. test scores, but I think we all have the feeling that it does exist. An example I can give is the following: I gave my program to a high I.Q. sixth grader. It was designed for someone with a high school education, since all of our employees at least have that. But this sixth grader went right through it. On this exposure example, she got all four answers right because she was studying fractions in school at the time, and she knew fractions cold. So I think it does tie in quite directly with what has been said.

This child was just someone who was interested in trying the program. I thought it would provide some useful information on what level students could complete the program and what they could get out of it.

DEESE: Of course, this points up the real advantage of having a program. You can pinpoint something like this. While, with a conventional course you might know that you are getting relatively poor performance on a general examination given at the completion of the course, or on examinations given throughout the course, you might have greater difficulty precisely pinpointing the difficulty.

GAGNE: Since you have raised this subject again, which interests me very much, I would like to make a comment on it. My remark agrees with a number of things that have been said, but perhaps says it in a little different way. First of all, I do not own a camera and I do not know very much about cameras. However, I sat here and made responses to these questions on exposures, and they are all right. I am not boasting about that, but I am asking a question. Why are they all right? What is the difference between me and your secretary, or the other people in the room who missed the questions? I did not have any practice. Now why is it that I was able to do it? I think the answer lies in this, which has been said a couple of times: I happen to have some subordinate knowledge which enabled me to acquire this new principle of exposure systems very readily. That is what a program should do. If you ask, then, why the secretaries did not do this, I would say, very simply, that it was because they did not have this subordinate knowledge. This is what should have been supplied in the program.

If you want me to identify what this is, I think it is, first, knowledge of how to translate one numerical scale into another. A second kind of subordinate knowledge I have has to do with the nature of a geometric scale in terms of fractions. Now you might say, that in itself involves some subordinate knowledge about fractions; I think it does. In other words, I think there is a whole knowledge structure which you do not have in your program and which the secretaries do not have. The problem of programing is to start where they are. I do not think you can find this out simply by giving a a test of arithmetic. I am not talking about general knowledge of arithmetic. I am talking about specific knowledge of these particular things. Now, when you include these in the program you can, by presenting a number of frames, achieve perfect accomplishment, as I did.

Cook: There are other things you can do, too, if you want to rationalize and motivate the learning of this inverse scale. You can go through a series of frames talking about filters and filter values so that an imagery is created which will support this difficult or dangerous inversion. It is often worth doing, even though it is not specifically true that you have filters there.

Comment: I think Don Cook used a word that is probably basic to learning by any method. That word is motivate. I think all of us here were motivated to get this concept. Regardless of the type of teaching that you do—whether it be the conventional method or programed learning— the subject must be motivated to learn, or he is not going to.

Bruce: The interesting thing to me, though, is that I showed this to a few people before I came down. The general reaction was that it would be ridiculous to try this particular example because it was too simple. It was felt that everybody in the group would get it 100% correct and would lose the idea of why secretaries had difficulties. I had exactly the same reaction from everybody that I got from Bob Gagne. Now the interesting fact is that not everybody in this group got it 100% correct, and this is not what I would call a low I.Q.

group! I think you come to the basic problem here that we have in education right from the start—what are these subordinate bits of information that each of us has? I must determine this anytime I have a class to teach, so I can select the best method of teaching. For this reason, the big thing that I see in programed learning is that it is on an individual basis. I can go from an individual to the source of his trouble. If a lot of individuals have a bit of trouble, then I am wrong. If one individual has a bit of trouble, then I can help that one individual.

GLASER: Bob Gagne's remarks imply something more which is probably not done enough. This is what I sometimes call assessing the entering repertoire. You have to know what the student has already learned so you can take him from there to where you want him to go. It is a special problem, but assessing the entering repertoire so that you know where you have started is important. I think your being afraid the example was too simple is also generally true. The more you program, the more you find that it is hard to make things too simple.

McNAMARA: As I understand it, Jim Bruce was using a linear program. In view of the presentation on revising the program and some of our general discussion, I would like to ask Bob Glaser to make a comment on how branching enters in here.

GLASER: The first comment I have to make is that I think the linear and branching furor is ridiculous. It is true that linear programing may have some more theoretical notions behind it than the other, but I think they both can be put into a similar framework. One method of responding does not have any more intrinsic value than the other. It depends on what you want to teach.

The other thing is that in our initial crude attempts at programing, we are writing programs that are intended for the average of a group, just as we build tests for the average of a group. I suppose that as we get more and more sophisticated, we will build tests which are specifically suited for individuals, rather than build tests for the large mass of people. Similarly, as the technology of programing increases and we learn to use machines again, getting them in proper perspective, we will make programs more and more individualized. I think the notion of branching will come up more and more; and I think more and more people will attempt to write branching programs. Of course, they are so much more complicated to write than linear ones. At this stage of the game, linear programing seems the easiest thing to do.

COOK: There are two related points in the last two things you said. The notion of assessing the entering behavior repertoire is important in knowing what you can assume. If, when you write a program frame by frame, you make notes on what you assume the entering repertoire to be, these notes will constitute, so to speak, your entrance requirements for the program. If you do this, you can test the program on people that you can screen using these entrance requirements. Then when you get validation data, you are validating the program and not what the people are bringing to it. At the same time, you have data in a form that will permit you, if you want to, to write several graded entry routines and give a diagnostic check list. If people do not have some of the entering repertoire, you can have small programs that precede the main line and feed into it. So for both research and practical purposes, it is an extremely important step.

DEESE: Another point can be made about this entering repertoire of behavior. Why are there variations? Take the simple-minded view that, at some time in the past, all the secretaries in this program had been exposed to fractions and had achieved some acceptable level of performance. And yet, if their ability with fractions was assessed at the time the program began, we would presumably find the behavior needed to support the concept to be learned was not present. Therefore, you would have to reteach what has been taught before. In other words, we assume there has been some forgetting. Then we teach the concept in the program and establish some criterion of acceptable level of performance. Are we then to assume that what has been taught in the program remains at this stable level. If not, what has gone wrong? Has there been a reforgetting of the supporting material which we had to teach first before we could teach the concept? In other words, is there something inherent about this material which makes it drop out and cause the concept to be lost? Or is the concept itself subject to the same problem

GAGNE: Could you tell us what the machine is like, in general? I assume that you are using film.

BRUCE: Yes, colored film. The machine contains 40 frames on a slide. The operator advances these on a rear projection viewer by pushing the button to indicate his response. When the correct response is shown, it advances to the next frame. These frames are alternately covered and shown, covered and shown. That is one kind of machine we use. Because of the difficulty we had in getting machines in quantity—because these were almost hand built—we went to a commercially available Recordak 310 Reader. We found that this works perfectly well, too. The big reason we went to the machine is the amount of paper that we were faced with in programing. It is phenomenal! It gets to be a real storage problem.

HOLT: I would like to comment on the teaching machines vs. programed books issue. It is probably easy to overgeneralize the findings in our study, although we think they probably pertain to similar types of machines. Our machine is pretty much like the Rheem-Califone Didak or the Foringer machine. However, I would like to relate an incident to you for which I am indebted to Bob Mager. He said, "I don't know why you people did that study comparing books and machines." I said, "What do you mean?" He said, "Well, you set up your program so that people could turn pages—this was the book form—and then you built a machine which essentially turned the pages. Why did you expect any difference?" Well, of course, my answer to this is we really did not, but that was why we did the study. As everyone here knows, I guess, two or three years ago there was quite a controversy about books and machines. Certain people said machines are essential and should be used. Others said no, machines are not important, what is important is the program. I have a strong notion that any machine which is simply a page-turner, and this includes the computer setups I have seen, is going to produce the same results.

The other point concerns this matter of a lot of paper. We have a lot of paper, too, in our program. But I really don't think it dawned on me until lately that it does not have to be that much paper. Our program will come down to the size, and in fact is going to be published in the size, of the English 2600 program. That's all the paper it is. We just did not use our paper very economically.

III

TRAINING OF PLANT OPERATORS

AND MAINTENANCE PERSONNEL *

L . H . O ' D O N N E L L †

BACKGROUND

Dr. Skinner's now famous article on teaching machines, published in SCIENCE magazine, was the "prompt" for du Pont's entry into the field of programed instruction. We were impressed by the implications. Apparently students could learn much more in much less time through programed instruction than they could learn in a conventional instruction class. They could do this without attending class as a group, and without the presence of an instructor.

* Portions of this chapter were published previously in the American Society of Mechanical Engineers' Paper Number 62-MPE-6 of March 29, 1962, and in "Reading Engineering Drawings," "Measurement for Installation and Construction Skills," "Plain Bearings," and "Pressure and Its Measurement." We wish to thank the American Society of Mechanical Engineers and Basic Systems, Inc., respectively, for permission to reprint them here.

† Engineering Service Division, Engineering Department, E. I. du Pont de Nemours & Co.

The evidence to support Dr. Skinner's conclusions appeared to us to be very limited but nevertheless valid. In mid-1959 we decided to investigate. I discussed the concepts of programed instruction with Dr. Skinner, Dr. Homme, Dr. Evans, Dr. Klaus, and several others in the field; spent an hour on one of Dr. Skinner's teaching machines at Harvard; briefly reviewed the programed textbook course in statistics at the University of Pittsburgh; completed a small part of the program on physics, developed at the American Institute for Research; and did a lot of reading in the field of experimental psychology. This investigation led us to the conclusion that programed instruction had the potential to increase the effectiveness and reduce the costs of our industrial training activities. Our management then authorized an experimental study to confirm this potential.

During 1959 and 1960 that was a formidable task. We could not use any of the experimental programs which had been prepared on academic subjects. Even if they could have been made available to us, they would not have been suitable for the type of training in which we were interested. We had to prove our conclusions with a programed instruction course on a topic directly related to industrial training, used in a typical industrial training situation. To do this, we first had to write the program.

In mid-1960 we selected "Reading Engineering Drawings" (1) as our topic. It is a traditional, widely used topic in the field of employee training.

I will not elaborate on the blood, sweat, and tears which

were expended in developing our twelve-hour program on "Reading Engineering Drawings." I will skip those details and go on to describe some of its contents. The figures on this and the following pages are examples of the content of the program.

Figure 1 indicates how the trainee learns to identify a "blind" hole. A very strong prompt insures the correct response. From material like that in Figure 2 the trainee learns one of the characteristics of a drawing of a blind hole. From Figure 3 the trainee learns to identify the

479.   A hole which does not go all the way through is called a "blind" hole.
        A hole in this part is called a _____ hole.

Figure 1

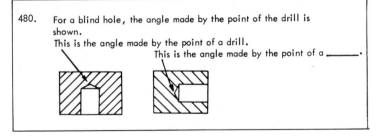

480.   For a blind hole, the angle made by the point of the drill is shown.
        This is the angle made by the point of a drill.
        This is the angle made by the point of a _____.

Figure 2

114 L. H. O'DONNELL

"depth" of a blind hole. In Figure 4 he uses his small bit
of new knowledge to identify the depth of two blind holes.

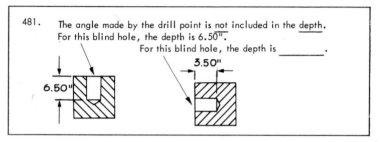

481. The angle made by the drill point is not included in the depth.
For this blind hole, the depth is 6.50".
For this blind hole, the depth is _____.

6.50"

3.50"

Figure 3

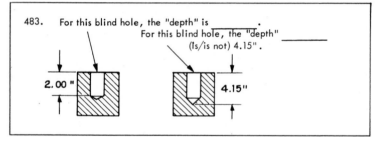

483. For this blind hole, the "depth" is _____.
For this blind hole, the "depth" _____
(Is/is not) 4.15".

2.00 "

4.15"

Figure 4

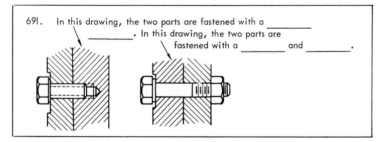

691. In this drawing, the two parts are fastened with a _____
_____. In this drawing, the two parts are
fastened with a _____ and _____.

Figure 5

The program continues to build new knowledge and becomes more and more complex as the trainee proceeds through it. Figure 5 illustrates a more complex bit of new knowledge for the trainee.

EXPERIMENTATION

In early 1961 we used our program in a controlled experiment. We selected twelve trainees, all of whom had a total lack of knowledge of the topic. A wide variation in age, aptitude, formal education, and prior experience existed among these men. That is typical of an industrial training situation.

Six of the trainees were assigned to a conventional instruction class, and a highly competent instructor was assigned to teach them how to read engineering drawings. The other six men, with a comparable range of aptitudes, were issued individual copies of our program and individual teaching machines. Each man proceeded independently, at his own pace, without supplementary material, and without the presence of an instructor.

One week after all of the trainees had completed their instruction we gave each man a comprehensive 3-hour examination. The results of the controlled experiment are summarized in Table I. Those who received programed instruction spent twenty-five per cent less time in learning the subject, and achieved significantly higher scores on the examination than those who received the conventional group instruction.

TABLE I

Programed Instruction vs. Conventional Instruction
"Reading Engineering Drawings"

	Programed Instruction Method	Conventional Instruction Method	Programed vs. Conventional
Avg. Man-Hrs. per Trainee	12.8	17.0	25% Less
Avg. Exam. Score	91%	81%	13% More

Of perhaps even greater significance was the range of achievement, as shown in Table II. Although there was wide variation in the amount of time required to complete the programed instruction course, the level of achievement was uniformly high. In the conventional instruction class, the wide variation in level of achievement was typical of the industrial training situation.

TABLE II

Programed Instruction vs. Conventional Instruction
"Reading Engineering Drawings"

	Experimental Group	Control Group
Range of Trainee Man-Hrs.	11.5-15.3	17.0-17.0
Range of Exam Scores	87.2%-97.6%	72.0%-94.0%

Our original optimism regarding programed instruction for industrial training was apparently justified. With programed instruction, we could increase significantly the effectiveness and reduce the. costs of our training activities.

OTHER DEVELOPMENTS

We recognized that our conclusion was still a rather broad generalization. There probably were several major limitations which we had not identified in our very restricted experimental study. Our management decided, however, to go ahead with the development of programs on other topics. We would try to identify the limitations which might exist, and overcome them if possible.

Since mid-1961 we have completed and validated five additional programs and have eight others close to completion. I would like to describe some of the features of these programs and the behavior which they are designed to establish.

"Measurements" (2) is the title of one of the completed and validated programs. It covers the measurement of angles and straight line distances, and describes the use of tools to perform these tasks. We deliberately designed this program to establish specific forms of non-verbal behavior. The trainee is to learn to use measuring tools correctly and efficiently.

On the following pages are examples of frames from the program on "Measurements." In Figure 6 the trainee reads a scale on a steel rule. Figure 7 illustrates how the trainee learns the correct way to place a steel rule to measure a diameter. In the frame in Figure 8, the trainee verbally measures a diameter. Somewhat similar treatment is given

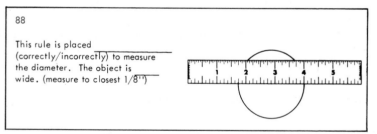

Figure 6

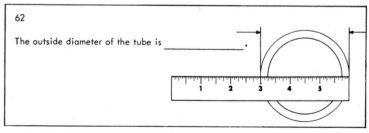

Figure 7

Figure 8

to the protractor, the combination set, and the micrometer in this 10-hour program. In our validation tests we found that the trainees could successfully monitor their non-verbal measurement behavior. With no instruction other than that received from the program they could use measuring tools correctly and efficiently.

We feel that there is a significant difference between the behavior established by the program on Reading Engineering Drawings, and that established by the program on Measurements. In the former we reinforced verbal behavior to establish the verbal behavior of reading drawings. In the latter we reinforced verbal behavior to establish the non-verbal behavior of taking measurements. Since the establishment of non-verbal behavior is very important to the field of industrial training, we feel that our experience with this program is most significant.

We have also completed and validated a 10-hour program on bearings (3) and an 18-hour program on pressure instrumentation (4). Examples of frames from the program on bearings are presented in Figures 9, 10, and 11.

A few frames from the program on pressure instrumentation are illustrated in Figures 12, 13, 14, and 15.

The programs on bearings and pressure instrumentation establish both verbal and non-verbal forms of behavior. The trainees can respond successfully to questions concerning these topics and can perform effectively certain job tasks relative to the "hardware" involved.

We have also designed programed instruction courses to train plant operators. I cannot describe the content of these programs for they are explicit to du Pont's manufacturing processes. I will, however, describe their general nature.

On the job, the plant operator must make highly com-

165

When metal breaks from repeated bending, it is called metal fatigue.

This wire broke from repeated bending because of _____ .

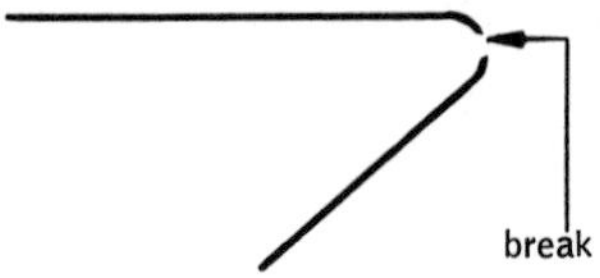

break

Figure 9

167

If a bearing lining suffers metal fatigue, the lining _____ (will/will not) break and pieces spall off.

Figure 10

189

When small pieces of a bearing lining break loose and flake off, it is a spalling type of failure.

Metal fatigue causes a " _____ " type of failure.

Figure 11

161

The curved surface of the liquid level is called a "meniscus."

This curved surface is called a _____ .

Figure 12

168

The liquid level in tube A is at 5 inches.

The liquid level in tube B is at what level?

_____

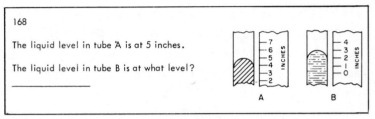

Figure 13

172

This meniscus is _____ (concave/convex).

The reading of 3 cm. is at the _____ (top/bottom) of the meniscus.

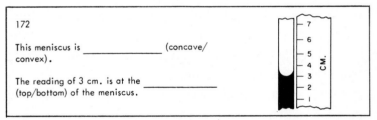

Figure 14

207

This manometer is graduated in _____ .

The manometer reading is _____ .

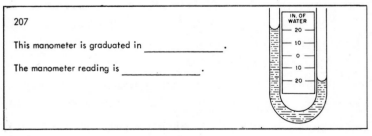

Figure 15

plex responses in the presence of very brief and very restricted stimuli. For example, the reading of a thermometer
can be the cause for opening and closing various valves,
turning on and turning off certain items of electrical equipment, adjusting the flow of certain materials, and many
other responses. Because of the size of the plant operation
involved, feedback to the operator for these responses may
be delayed for many minutes, even hours. Due to this delay
in feedback, the plant operator must carefully control his
actions in order not to overshoot the desired condition for
the process.

In our programs for plant operators we establish strong
verbal behavior relative to the events that occur during
the operation, and to the conditions under which these
events occur. We teach the trainee to diagram the entire
operation and to sketch the internal arrangement of the
process equipment. We also have him identify the variables
that exist in the operation and learn their interrelationships.
With this strong verbal behavior, the trainee can effectively
monitor and control his own nonverbal actions on the job.

Bearings, measurements, pressure instrumentation, plant
operations, and engineering drawings all fall within the
category of subjects for training hourly-paid employees. We
are equally interested in subjects of a more technical nature
and have developed the first part of a program on analog
computation (5). This program is related to the analysis
of engineering problems through simulation with an analog
computer. The first part is concerned with the events that
occur in analog simulation and with the conditions under

which these events occur. Subsequent parts of this program will be concerned with the tasks involved in engineering analysis.

While developing the program on analog simulation we became aware of a very difficult problem. Because of the abstract nature of the subject, the behavior to be established in the trainee by this program is largely internal, mental in nature. The expert possesses this behavior, but finds that he cannot readily identify it explicitly and in detail. This difficulty in full identification of the behavior involved in highly abstract subjects may prove to be one limitation to the use of programed instruction for all industrial training tasks. We expect to learn more about it as we get further along with the other parts of this program.

APPLICATIONS

In our applications of programed instruction we have found a wide variation in the time required to complete a program. This time-to-complete factor does not correlate with age, formal education, aptitude test score, or any other variable that we can identify. Because we have no means for identifying the time factor, we have always had each trainee proceed independently, at his own pace, with his individual program. We feel that this procedure is a critical requirement for the success of programed instruction. We believe that an externally imposed time restriction would introduce one of the conditions which now hampers the effectiveness of the conventional group instruction class.

We have also found that within our population the age, the formal education, and the prior experience of the trainee do not correlate with level of achievement in programed instruction. Each program does, of course, have certain minimum prerequisites. A certain reading ability and a certain proficiency with mathematics are typical of minimum prerequisites. Once these have been met, however, we find no restrictions on the effectiveness of the programed instruction. If a particular program is pertinent to the job requirements of a trainee who has the minimum prerequisites, we permit him to complete the program. We do not restrict arbitrarily the use of a program on the basis of age, formal education, or prior experience of the trainee. In fact, the age of the men who have taken our programs ranges between 23 years and 61 years, and formal education ranges between completion of fourth grade and achievement of a Ph.D. degree.

We usually conduct programed instruction on company time. The trainee is relieved of his normal job duties during certain periods of time to permit him to work on his program. The length of time per day has varied from one hour to four hours depending upon the particular work situation. We have had men spend from 8:00 a.m. until 12:00 noon on their programs, with a ten minute break at 10:00 a.m. Although these men had no objection to that rather strenuous schedule, we feel that about two hours per day is less fatiguing and, therefore, more efficient.

We have had occasions in which the trainees work on their programs on their own time. In that situation we usually set a date in the future on which the man will return the program and take the criterion test. We believe that this distant stimulus encourages effective use of the programed instruction provided.

SUMMARY

In conclusion, I would like to repeat that we have found programed instruction to be valuable and effective for training plant operators, maintenance personnel, and other employees. We plan to continue the development of programs pertinent to our training needs.

Summarized below are what appear to us to be the key advantages of programed instruction for industrial training:

1. Competent "instructors" (i.e., "programs") are *always* available.

2. An operating plant *need* take just one man off the job for training at any one time.

3. As few as one man at a time can be given training, assuming the program is available.

4. "Fast" men can learn more in a given period of time.

5. "Slow" men can learn, if given the time to do so.

6. Industrial training can be accomplished at a lower cost with higher effectiveness.

BIBLIOGRAPHY

1. *Reading Engineering Drawings* by L. H. O'Donnell, Engineering Department, E. I. du Pont de Nemours & Co, Inc., Wilmington, Delaware, Copyright 1961.

2. *Measurements* by R. S. Pease, Textile Fibers Department, E. I. du Pont de Nemours & Co., Inc., Wilmington, Delaware, Copyright 1961.

3. *Plain Bearings* by C. R. Taylor, Textile Fibers Department, E. I. du Pont de Nemours & Co., Inc., Wilmington, Delaware, Copyright 1961.

4. *Pressure and Its Measurement* by M. A. Sayland, Textile Fibers Department, E. I. du Pont de Nemours & Co., Inc., Wilmington, Delaware, Copyright 1961.

5. *Analog Computation—Part I* by L. H. O'Donnell and J. P. Laird, Engineering Department, E. I. du Pont de Nemours & Co., Inc., Wilmington, Delaware, Copyright 1961.

DISCUSSION

DR. JAMES DEESE: I would like to comment on two things. First, I would like to say that I am probably the only one here who is not directly concerned with programed instruction research. I am here, I suppose, because I am an experimental psychologist in the area of learning. I would, however, like to comment a little bit on some research on programing which I know about. It complements what Mr. O'Donnell has told us about the variety of material which it is possible to bring into the concept of programing, and how, at the same time—as I think is very much implied by what Mr. O'Donnell has presented—the concepts and ideas of programing have to be expanded.

At the Johns Hopkins Hospital, there is a research program on teaching candidates for the MD degree how to read a "heart sentence." This has always been a great difficulty in teaching students. There is now a program of research which is built on a certain amount of traditional instruction and then branches out into the specific problems to be taught in the diagnosis of heart disease. First of all, as you know, there are different locations. The relationship has to be taught between these locations and the functions and the causes which produce the heart sounds at different locations. This is a verbal

127

program which can be taught by the kind of techniques which are traditionally used in programed instruction. But later the students must learn to identify the sounds which are made at different locations, and the sounds which are made in different normal and pathological conditions. One of the techniques in the program—I don't know if this is the only one or the best one—is always to give students pairs of items. A sound is produced on a tape recorder—initially these were real heart sounds—followed by a statement that this is an example of a specific sound at a specific location. Then a second sound is presented with the statement that it is an example of a particular sound at a particular location. The student is then given one of these pairs again and asked to identify the source and the nature of the condition. The pairs are systemically varied to provide a very large number of discrimination trials (because that is what it amounts to) for each student. One of the problems that the program uncovered was that the student's criteria for judging various sounds was very poor. This is an art as much as anything else, and it led to spectrographic treatment and attempted artificial simulation of the heart sounds by spectrographic records. In addition to the non-verbal skills which Mr. O'Donnell discussed, therefore, even discrimination tasks of this sort, which are very critical, can be programed.

Now I would like to comment briefly on what I regard as the two problems in the analysis of programs. Part of this is in connection with things that I have said before. I believe the major advantage of a program is that it enables you to take a program apart. That is to say, the program is not intuitively put together, in the sense of no one having an objective record of what precisely is being said or being taught at any given point in the program. Therefore, it can be pulled apart and studied analytically. We ask then, what are the conditions which, granted this analytic power, make for good or poor programs? As an experimental psychologist, one of the things that would occur to me if I were in this business would be to design bad programs deliberately. Now I suspect that this is not a feasible enterprise for people involved in training research in industry, but it is this sort of basic research which would contribute useful information to our understanding of the elements that go into the construction of good programs.

From the early discussions, and from the theoretical papers, we all know about the psychological concepts which have gone into the design of programs, such as the effect of reinforcement and the nature of attending or responding. The latter is perhaps one of the things which, because of the nature of the traditional lecture-demonstration, we do not know very much about. Because it forces responding to each element, the program demands a greater degree of responding to what is being presented than the lecture-discussion method. Perhaps, in view of this, we ought to wonder why it is that lecture-demonstrations turn out to be as good as they do in comparison with programed techniques. Perhaps our programs are unnecessarily long and detailed. This suggests that, given this very considerable advantage in a programed presentation, we ought to look for ways of making programs very much more efficient than they are.

There is, of course, a factor touched upon by Dr. Holt this morning, which I think must be present in Mr. O'Donnell's research, namely, the presence of the Hawthorne* effect in studies on programed learning. If so, we ought to get some idea of the extent to which it is present because this is the sort of thing that, with the passing of time, ought to begin to disappear. As programed instruction becomes very nearly universal, programs ought to decrease in effectiveness a little bit to the extent that they are currently influenced, if indeed they are, by something like the Hawthorne effect.

Finally, another great advantage of programs is that they demand that we be explicit. They almost force us to be explicit, with respect to criteria. At each step, the question is raised for us whether a particular item in a training course is suitable for programing, whether it should be taught at all, or whether this is information which we specifically want to be taught. This is, I think, the most significant by-product of the design of pro-

---

* Editor's Note: The Hawthorne effect as used here means the extent to which the novelty of the technique contributes to the positive results obtained with programed learning. The name originated with the first industrial psychology experiments done more than 30 years ago at the Hawthorne works of Western Electric Co.

grams, the way in which it forces us to be explicit about what we want to teach. This means that sooner or later we are going to be faced with what are now a lot of sticky and difficult questions in psychology. Do we really want to teach concepts, or do we want to teach people how to exemplify, how to perform correctly without ever really understanding the concept? I will use the language analogy here that most people in the world speak grammatically, in the sense that they speak according to the rules of communication and the culture in which they live, but most people in the world cannot describe or specify the grammatical concepts which are necessarily there and which govern the language that they use. So questions of the extent to which we want to teach people through programs to identify and name general concepts and ideas, and the extent to which we want to teach them to be able to use examples of these concepts correctly, can be raised within the context of the analytical approach which programed learning makes possible.

In the laboratory, we have never faced one of the problems which people now face in building programs; our criteria are always explicitly built in for us. That is, we have people learn precisely what we want them to learn. This has never been a problem in the experimental laboratory. In an experimental study of learning, you design your tasks and you have complete freedom to design the task to produce precisely what you want to produce. You can, therefore, study the single variable of effectiveness in the laboratory, or the rate at which the subject achieves the criterion which one specifies. Before you can attack that problem—the rate at which people approach given criteria in real, applied training programs—you must first identify the criteria for which you want to aim. Otherwise, a lot of very expensive and detailed research on programing may go for naught. That is finally the thing which I think programing research will force us to do, that is, to be increasingly more explicit about the particular criteria or outcomes of the training program which you want to produce.

GAGNE: I had a question that occurred to me about one item that Mr. O'Donnell presented, the one which tells how to measure the diameter of a round object. It states how to do it, that is, it states that you put the measuring instrument on the center, and then the frame goes on to state that, in this picture, "the rule is placed in the _____ of the object." What the individual is required to do in this case is to make the response "center."

Now, what I am wondering is, why try to establish this verbal response? This relates to some of Jim Deese's remarks. I don't know the answer. But why not, after making that same statement, get the trainee merely to choose a drawing indicating the correct method of using the instrument to measure the diameter. Now, all I am saying is that in the first instance, if you want to be specifically Skinnerian about this, the individual is acquiring this verbal response "center," or is using it, I guess. In the second instance, he is pointing to or identifying the correct placement of the measuring instrument in order to determine its diameter. Is there a choice to be made here? Is one of these approaches better than the other? If so, why or why not?

O'DONNELL: It's a very interesting problem. Let me say one thing. Ahead of this particular item in the program, we make sure that he knows what a diameter is. In this particular example I gave you, you may have noticed that there is a rule, namely, that to measure the diameter of a round object, the edge of the rule must intersect the center of the object. So in this particular frame we give him the rule as a verbal stimulus and he fills in the blank "center." As a matter of actual fact, the sort of thing that you cited in your example is in our program, but in a more difficult problem. We have the thing intersected in more places. The first introduction to this concept of measuring the diameter of a round object, however, consists of giving a specific rule and a specific example of that particular rule, and no other. From there we make sure that he will generalize the idea of measuring the diameter of a round object. The way we do this is through a variety of examples, some of which are correct, some of which are incorrect, in which he must differentiate as well as generalize.

GAGNE: So that it is not a matter of one method vs. another. You have both of them in the program.

O'DONNELL: But we do specifically give him the verbal response first.

HUGHES: Apropos of this point, I guess the question would

relate to what Jim Deese was saying. Is this a point at which we can make the program more efficient? In other words, are both processes necessary? Does he have to verbalize the concept as well as be able to apply the concept? This might be one of the areas to investigate to determine if the preparation of programs can be made more efficient in shorter periods of time.

DEESE: How many items of this sort must you have? Now this is supposedly a fairly easy discrimination, and one ought to be able to arrive at some general rules about how many kinds of choices you must give somebody to insure he will learn discriminations of a given difficulty.

O'DONNELL: I don't know whether anyone has an answer to that question. In Figure 8 we not only had a round object, but also the diameter of a tube which had no center. This, of course, is a criterion frame. The trainee knows that this is the test of what we were talking about when we told him how to measure the diameter of a round object. Now I really would like to have some way to determine how many examples you have to give to teach this? Where does this information come from?

GLASER: You are getting at some extremely important problems that the experimental psychologist has, the problems of practice, review and repetition. How many frames do you have to present? Right now we all play it by ear. I think now we have a really good situation in which we can begin to study the amount of review and repetition in relation to a drop in the retention curve.

This is the kind of thing that we are doing now in some of my research, actually trying to build certain programs in order to test limits of the amount of review and repetition.

An answer to Bob Gagne's question is related to what John Hughes said in regard to efficiency, and also to the entering repertoire that the person brings to the program. Sometimes you can use the word "center" and sometimes you cannot. Whether you may ask the student to discriminate or supply the word "center" depends on what response he has available when he begins the program.

GAGNE: You mean that if someone does not know the word "center," you need an item in the program which enables him to use the word "center" because you are going to use it further on.

O'DONNELL: More important. He may have a vague idea of center, but we cannot afford that vagueness. He needs an explicit understanding of "center."

HUGHES: Does he really need an understanding of the word "center," or is it merely a hole somewhere in the object?

O'DONNELL: No. He needs a very explicit understanding of "center."

CHILDS: Do you tell him what center means? Are there some frames defining this?

O'DONNELL: No, as a matter of fact, we do not.

CHILDS: You expect him to know what center is?

O'DONNELL: We expect that he comes to this with a vague idea of what center is.

Question: Do you show him how to find the center in a circle?

O'DONNELL: No, you don't run into trouble. The man takes a steel rule and moves it up until he gets the maximum measurement. As a matter of fact, you use this technique to find the center, too. We do teach him to do that with a steel rule.

McNAMARA: I am intrigued by some of these comments. It appears that now that we have programed instruction, we can determine or study how much practice and repetition are required. It just occurred to me that the people who investigate learning have been doing this for the last fifty years or so. For example, how many times must a person have exposure to the rule "i before e," before he knows it? I thought these things had been studied for some time. I don't see why, now that we have programed instruction, we are in a better position to study things like that.

DEESE: Well, these things have been studied for some time. This relates to my point about the laboratory. Really what the laboratory student of learning has had all along are programs of various sorts, precisely in this sense. That is to say, he constructs material which has certain properties. He just does not say, now we want to teach people arithmetic. He will say now I am going to construct some material which will have thus and such properties. I will then study the effect of these properties on how well the material is retained, or how long it takes to learn, or whatever. But, until now, the experimental psychologist has never faced this problem in a situation in which somebody is taught something for a practical reason. That is to say, you have some criterion for constructing materials other than your own inherent interest in the way learning proceeds. This is what makes the difference. Until the advent of programing we had very little information about retention with materials in such subjects as arithmetic, spelling, grammar.

McNamara: Hasn't the educational psychologist, rather than the experimental psychologist, had this practical viewpoint?

Deese: No, because what the educational psychologists have done, by and large, is to study the different gross techniques of teaching, using their control-experimental comparison technique. The classical study is the old Gates' study of repetition vs. reading. Remember, he had four or five groups of people that read both nonsense material and prose material for various periods of time. Or there are the studies that I mentioned earlier, the Brownell studies on subtraction, in which there are two different methods of subtraction, equal additions and some other one. You study how fast students learn by these two different methods when taught, not by any specific item-by-item program, but generally by teachers using one method or the other. You then compare the outcomes of these two methods. I think that until very recently, with very few exceptions, educational psychology has not faced the detailed construction of items which has gone into programed learning. Experimental psychologists have studied this detailed construction, item by item, but always for material which is of no extrinsic interest to people with practical training problems.

GLASER: I think the kind of behavior studied in the O'Donnell paper is very interesting. I want to point out that here the notions of a constructed response, or a discrimination response, or a multiple choice response have been brought up quite naturally without getting into the usual whose-theory-is-right-type of debate. We ask the questions, where do we want to go, and what do we need to get there?

The thing that intrigues me, and I think it is something that becomes very interesting when you program for practical training, is the use of multiple-choice responding for the eventual production of constructed responses. You keep making the point that someone can monitor his own behavior once he learns to discriminate, and this is a very interesting point. You may not have to get students to produce the behavior. Sometimes it is tough to produce the behavior, and it is easier to evaluate a multiple-choice response by machine. The point I am trying to make is that you can build up a history of discrimination, and at the end of it students can generalize to a written response. Adults—and it may not be true of children—if they learn to discriminate between two words can, after such discrimination, produce one of the words without ever having produced it in the course of a program. They can type it, they can do lots of things with it if they can just learn to discriminate it. In a program, you do not have to construct a response all the time. This is particularly striking in some of the work that comes out of Jim Evans' thesis and his later work. He taught children to discriminate among the numbers from 1 to 10. These children could not write these numbers. They were taught only to discriminate the numbers, using a multiple-choice procedure. At the end of this history of discrimination, they could, without any other practice, write the numbers. The point I am trying to make is that in your own program preparation, you might be quite successful just using a multiple-choice technique for some more complicated responses to which you eventually want people to generalize. You, of course, have to be careful, because we don't know the limits of generalization.

O'DONNELL: I might add that in our engineering drawing program, the trainee makes no sketches at all. He simply reads everything and writes things down. In the examination we gave our trainees, they had to make a free hand sketch, and they did it exactly right.

HUGHES: The Evans study that Bob mentioned was a very fascinating one. I was curious to know, however, what these children might have been doing when they were not under Evans's supervision. Could their parents have been showing them how to write numbers? How do we know that these children were not practicing these responses somewhere else?

GLASER: I am just saying that it is very intriguing for us to study the generalization between one response mode and another. If we find that responses are highly generalizeable, then we can use the simplest one and the one most easily incorporated into our program.

GAGNE: In my previous comments, I was not, of course, raising the issue of multiple-choice responses, but I am glad that this did come up. Just take these two different ways of responding, verbally and by actually doing something. I realize that you did not do this in your program. But if I constructed a program of this type, what would I expect? I would expect that, in the first instance, if I asked the question, "Where should you put the ruler to measure a round object?" the trainee would be able to say "center." In the second instance, I would expect that if I said to him, "Put your ruler on the object to measure its diameter," he would be able to do it. Now, in other words, to make it very simple, I would expect that the first man would be learning to "talk" a good job, and the second one would be learning to do it. I don't know the extent to which this question arises.

HUGHES: This brings up the question of how this whole thing should be conceptualized. Should the trainee be told to put the ruler on the center of the object, or should he be told merely to maximize the measurement of the ruler? This would be another way of verbalizing the same thing. And why bother with the center at all? There are probably a number of different ways of programing this concept.

O'DONNELL: This is one of the nice things about programed instruction. You have this freedom.

KNIGHT: I think this is what happens when you first start programing. At least, I found in my case, you usually stick to one type and you are pretty restrictive in what you are doing. You are either straight Skinnerian or straight Crowder without any mixing of the two. As you go along, however, you finally open up the field and you throw in anything that you think will help the situation. What I have done is to use a linear approach. In my revisions, however, I have used discriminations involving multiple-choice responses, and I also have them not only write the responses in, but draw sketches, name parts, and make other types of responses. The field is wide open. I think the more variety you have, the better.

O'DONNELL: I suspect there is a real limit, perhaps in the programer rather than anything else. In the development of these programs, we try to identify the variables that exist in a particular concept, no matter what size it is. We try to identify these variables and make sure we cover them. Take the example of placing that ruler somewhere else on the object. This was one factor we were well aware of, and this is in the program.

CHILDS: Larry, several of your frames looked as if they were two paragraphs rather than a continuation of the last sentence after the first. I was wondering why this was done.

O'DONNELL: To improve the quality of the stimulus. Anything we can do to improve the quality of the stimulus we feel is a plus. We do not want to make it tough for the trainee to read or to discriminate. We do not want to teach him to read. We do this deliberately. We start every sentence that way mechanically, and we make it easy to read. We do not write it as a paragraph. Even if it is only two sentences, they are separated.

Comment: Maybe some of you have seen this program on learning how to read a micrometer. This is a series of four small books. We have ordered some of these and given them to a few fellows who are in our machine shop who had experience or who are just starting. It took them anywhere from one to four hours to read these books. Then we handed them a micrometer, and said, "Okay, now read this." There was only one out of the group at that point who could read a micrometer. Then we asked the foreman, "How do you normally teach them to read a micrometer and how long will it take you?" The answer was, "I can teach a man in fifteen minutes how to read a micrometer." I think that this points up what you want to accomplish in your training. If you want to teach a conceptual idea, as John Hughes points out, the trainee may only be able to verbalize it. The fellow who reads this program on the micrometer can get the right answers all the way through, but when he gets through he still cannot read a micrometer. Perhaps an improvement might be to expand the program with some sample problems and let the trainee have a micrometer with him while he is reading the books. As the course goes on, he then has the occasion to use it.

O'DONNELL: You have just pointed out a problem that we have to face up to. People say, "Oh, I can teach that in half an hour." Or, "I can teach that in fifteen minutes." It sounds very good, but it is really not true. If you looked at those books pretty closely, you will find, for example, that in going through that course, the trainee learns the name of every part of a micrometer, and all of the sophisticated parts, things that I'm sure a foreman does not teach his trainees. The comparison is really unfair, although we wrote a program ourselves for this. We did not want to use that particular program that you are talking about simply because we thought a lot of it was unnecessary. So we wrote a program ourselves.

Question: In your program, did you actually have a micrometer in front of the trainees so that they could practice?

O'DONNELL: No.

CHILDS: The diagrams that Dr. Blyth used in his program seemed to be very clear and I would not think that they need a micrometer.

O'DONNELL: You do not. This is another part of this business of monitoring the behavior. After working through these illustrations, there is no question about picking one up, reading it, and everything else. We found no problem of translating from the illustrations to the hardware. It's just a case of the content of that program. This is really something that should be thought of. What does the man learn in that period of time? It's not fair to say micrometer, one hour. This equation is not fair, frankly.

GLASER: Don, how have you handled non-verbal behavior, such as making drawings or manipulations of some kind?

COOK: It all depends on what, using Skinner's terminology, we have come to call the grain of the repertoire that you can assume. You can ask people to make sketches, for example, of electrical diagrams, because anybody can do this. It does not require skill in shading. But when you get to biological diagrams where you want to shade and indicate depth, etc., then you begin to have a lot of trouble. If you want them to do that, you have to put in frames that explicitly generate that behavior. We have done some of that in a few medical programs, but not many, because we usually have not needed to. We have experimented with designing programs that go with kits. We have one in the electricity of magnetism in which there are instructions such as "Do this and what happens?" and the answer frame says, "The wire burned up." That is actually how it begins. Then it says, "Take a second wire out of the kit." This is very effective. You will note that with a discrimination sequence like this, one could call it multiple-choice, and certainly it is. However, at least in our shop, these are designed so that if the frame works out right, mistakes are not made. This is still the kind of programing in which we are not counting on the corrective effect of mistakes. First you establish the positive instance, then you introduce the negative instance that is very far away, and then you might ask for a verbalization, such as why is this not a such and such, why is this also not a such and such? Then you begin moving up the generalization gradient until finally you are getting fine discriminations, hopefully without error. It's a lot of fun to design those sequences, if you can do it.

HOLT: A different kind of question, Larry. I'm not sure if you have covered this. Your firm has produced a large number of programs. Who wrote the programs? By that I mean, what kind of people, under what kind of administrative circumstances?

O'DONNELL: That's a good question. In general, what has happened is that someone from a line organization has been detached from his current assignment and assigned to this activity for some period of time (6 months, a year, 2 years). He has a new job assignment. These men are, with one exception, not training people. They are men who have competent backgrounds in the subject. I work with them primarily to get across the art of programed instruction, as it applies to their particular subject. I'm sure that other people have had the same problem. The expert has some difficulty in describing what his expertise is, and he needs help here. This has been the way we have approached this in our company.

HOLT: Then, in a way, you have a kind of programing center?

O'DONNELL: No, we do not. These men remain at their plant site; all but one man is at a plant. We always manage to get the man an office with a door on it—that is always essential—but he remains at his particular plant center. The reason we have taken this particular approach is that we feel that immediate feedback to the programer is very essential. He has to have some guys on whom to try out the program just as soon as possible. If we bring him into a center, the company structure being what it is, this center would probably be removed from the industrial plant site. Then we could not have the trainees, the guinea pigs. I might say that this has complicated our problem. It has dispersed it, at least.

HOLT: Let me ask, if your trial subjects could be made available, would you like to have these programers together?

O'DONNELL: I'm sure that it would be more efficient.

HOLT: Do you give them a little training course ahead of time?

O'DONNELL: Well, this is where inefficiency enters into it, I suspect. I start off by possibly spending a full week with the man, and then come back two weeks later and spend a couple more days. If possible, group meetings are held. There might be three or four men that meet at one site for that period of time, and then they go back to their original sites. An efficiency problem sometimes arises when a guy gets into trouble with his program or with identifying the terminal behavior that he wants to establish. There is nobody to talk to. This is a delay factor, something that we have not solved yet.

MCNAMARA: I was wondering if you had any figures or estimates on how long it takes to produce these programs?

O'Donnell: Three man-days of programer time per hour of completed program.

Childs: What do you consider an hour of program?

O'Donnell: One hunded frames.

McNamara: In other words, a man can write one hundred frames in three days?

O'Donnell: No, he can do more than that in three days. He writes them, illustrates them, tests them, evaluates them, gets them typed, and everything else.

Bruce: Three man-days would be twenty-four hours. That would be approximately four frames an hour.

Hughes: The usual figures quoted are one to two frames an hour. Larry's are at a much more accelerated rate than that.

Bruce: How do you do it, Larry?

O'Donnell: I think we do it by paying attention to experimental psychology. My contacts in this field keep asking me, as a chemical engineer, how can you effectively design something without an understanding of the principle? I can't approach this thing, unless I have some real idea of the concept that I am working with. I think this is the real answer. Perhaps a happy marriage. Psychologists have a field, and I think chemical engineers have a field. I suspect that there is a happy marriage here. I think Skinner himself said that this is an engineering task, but it is an engineering task with an understanding and application of the principles of experimental psychology. That is as close as I can come to a definition, but frankly, this is really the key. Every

time you approach a new subject, the real key is your
approach. Once you get on the ball, one hundred
frames every three days is easy. You do not take your
training manual and write your frames from your training manual. This is totally destructive. We stopped that
a long time ago.

BRUCE: Is it one hundred frames in three days or four
frames an hour after you have—what we call—story-
boarded it, or is it from scratch?

O'DONNELL: It is from scratch. In other words, that figure
covers the end product that has been trial run.

McNAMARA: Looking at some of your frames with these
illustrations, I am wondering whether you work from
books or training manuals which already have a lot of
this material in pretty good shape.

O'DONNELL: We do not totally disregard the training manual, maybe only 90% of it. There is one thing that
perhaps I have been too general about. This program
on analog computation, believe me, took a lot more than
three days to write a hundred frames. It is the structure
of the subject, I suspect. In many areas, the structure
seems clear, and you can approach it right off without
any problem. But when we got hold of that difficult
one, we got the experts together and no one knew how
to approach it.

McNAMARA: Jim, it seems to me that some of the things
that you have programed are fairly close to what Larry
has programed, aren't they? I mean the kind of material.

BRUCE: The closest one is, of course, the slide rule.

McNAMARA: Do you have any estimates of how long that took you?

BRUCE: We were still in the spectrum of two to three frames per hour. We never got up any further. In fact, I have been looking at three frames per hour almost as a sound barrier. We have not hit four frames on anything we have programed.

O'DONNELL: Is it an average that you are talking about?

BRUCE: I am talking about the interval from the time the fellow starts with the manual until he has a validated program that we can use. We are running one to two frames per hour on the average.

GAGNE: I wanted to ask Larry a little more pensive question about this matter of how he gets started. He said a minute ago that they throw the training manual away, that is, discard it. What do you start with?

O'DONNELL: This is a good question. Our answer is, we don't care. You start wherever you want to start, and we don't care because you can back up; you can go forward; you can go in any direction. The solution to this particular problem we learned by experience. We spent a week trying to decide where we were going to start a particular program. This is totally non-productive. We finally got to the point of a total impasse. We then said, all right, we will start here and we won't worry about whether that's the place to start. And we took it from there on. I think this is the answer.

BRUCE: I think that this is all right, but first you have to find the object that this batch of frames is going to teach.

O'DONNELL: No. We define our terminal behavior. Terminal behavior, not only for this frame.

BRUCE: I am saying that you have to define the objective. I didn't say this frame. I mean this series of frames or this batch of frames. You have to define that objective. If you do not start there, as Dick Knight knows very well, you really get buried in the mire.

COOK: What is the maximum number of frames ahead of the ones already tested that you have let a program go?

O'DONNELL: Maybe one hundred, two hundred.

COOK: That's it. It is a question of designing a social system.

O'DONNELL: This is one of our problems with the approach to the training manual. I don't quite know how to say this and I am probably putting it in the wrong frame, but I think the experimental psychologist has a phrase for this. I think that the training manual is written as an end in itself. I don't think that this is the behavior you are looking at. It is somebody's behavior, but it isn't the behavior that you want to establish. This is what we have to identify, not the content of the training manual and not breaking it down into small steps. We don't even approach it this way.

GAGNE: I don't understand. What is it that is wrong with the training manual?

O'DONNELL: Well I'll give you an example. We want a man to use a steel rule correctly, to measure the diameter of round objects. Here is terminal behavior. What is involved? He sets his steel rule up there to make sure it intersects the center, that is terminal behavior—that's it right there.

GAGNE: Is that what is in the training manual?

O'DONNELL: Oh, no. The training manual takes three pages to say this.

Comment: What he is saying is that he does a task analysis and that the training manual is constructed without this in mind, apparently. The manual has content validity or face validity, but nothing to do with the actual behavior.

O'DONNELL: It is typical of textbooks.

KNIGHT: I think that Larry does have a good point about getting started. Jim has a point, too, in his mentioning that, of course, you do need to know your objectives or terminal behavior. But the thing with a lot of people, especially beginning programers, is to get them started in anything new. You can sit around and read about it, and how to do it, but you'll never get anywhere until you actually sit down and try to do something. You can start on a program, even if you don't know all the final objectives in the program. At least get started. Then you get a feeling for the whole subject material, and you can back up and write out exactly what you want to tell. The important thing is to start doing it.

O'DONNELL: I guess so, I think we found a lot of bad writing habits, too. When they write things down, they are not really being very precise about behavior. Often I wonder, where did that come from? They have to stop that. The programer spends a lot of time backing and filling, unless he blocks that reaction. A lot of the background of his writing habits really has to be blocked.

GAGNE: You think it is advantageous, in other words, in

writing each frame, for the writer to have in mind what kind of behavior this frame is going to estabish. Otherwise, he might write something which he is not very sure of.

O'DONNELL: As soon as they start looking out the window, this is a mistake.

McNAMARA: You mention this supervisory training material that you wrote. Do you find that you can get the same rate of production with this area?

O'DONNELL: Not quite, but it was surprisingly good. It was much better than the analog program. In supervisory training I think production was running about 75 to 80 frames every three days.

DEESE: How did you define your terminal behavior in the supervisory program?

O'DONNELL: In this particular case, there is a body of knowledge on what is correct and what is not correct in terms of the responses of the supervisor to a particular situation, how he should treat his boys, etc. This is it. Frankly, in some cases, that is still pretty vague. Our answer to that question was to have a programer who has a pretty high level position and has been with the company for 30 years. He knows.

DEESE: Specifically, in any kind of simple operation, you know pretty much all the characteristics and all the operations which are necessary to complete a job. But when you come to write a program in some area like this, supervisory training, do you know that your program is in any sense a complete one, one that can completely train somebody to do a particular job?

O'DONNELL: We are pretty well convinced that it is a partial one. This is intuitive.

Comment: There is another way of asking that same question relating to supervisory vs. other jobs. You can teach a guy how to read a micrometer in one plant, and you can transfer that to another plant quite readily. But, take a guy who is a programer, who has had programing experience in a given plant with given problems and given kinds of responses between the employee and the supervisor. His program may work fine for that particular situation. But take the program to another plant and try it out; see the different reactions that you are going to get.

O'DONNELL: This is what we do routinely. As a matter of fact, we never do the trial run at the same plant.

GLASER: You also have to define your students' entering behavior. You have to make some assumptions on what they know, or else you have to keep backing up until you hit a base, don't you?

O'DONNELL: Yes, we do, very definitely. Some one pointed out (I think Don did) about keeping a record as you are going along. In some cases where we define this entering repertoire in beginning to write the program, we do this. In other cases, such as the blueprint reading program, for example, we start it off with the assumption that the man is not able to do any mathematical operations whatsoever. This is traditionally where we like to place this. That problem is one that we do not want to get hung on. These programs were intended for use without an instructor, with nobody to answer questions. And so, to give us a fighting chance, we have to be sure that we set the stage properly. The guy has to have these minimum prerequisites.

CHILDS: Larry, you said that in your indoctrination program of these line personnel who write programs, you worked with them. Specifically, what do you do? How do you work with them?

O'DONNELL: Oh, that is a long story. I don't know whether I can outline it or not. I follow programing concepts. I give them examples of the rules, and I reinforce them every time they do it.

CHILDS: Do they read other programs? Do you show them good and bad frames?

O'DONNELL: Yes, definitely. You cannot talk about these concepts unless you give examples. I've found this is a fast way to get it across. Be sure you cover the examples of what you are talking about. That can be done efficiently by the use of other programs. You can have him identify characteristics of programs. Some routines that we have set up we find are efficient. They work. Perhaps the program is not a Cadillac, but it will be a good program. What I'm saying is that you will find some routines repeated through our programs, because we set them up. For example, we traditionally run into this. You have to teach the trainee the names of the parts. We have a routine for this, and this we almost put in a slot and push the button, because we have a way to do this that we think is really efficient.

McNAMARA: I think that we all are astounded at the productivity at duPont. I wonder if there are any other aspects of the material that Larry covered that you would like to discuss.

PETER: Larry, I don't think you gave us examples of your programing in the supervisory-subordinate area. I wonder if it was because it seems to be much harder to visualize. How do you define your terminal behavior, for example? I can understand the terminal behavior of a program on measuring the diameter of a tube, but I have a little more trouble seeing how you would define your terminal behavior in supervisory-subordinate relations. I wonder if you could explore this a little bit. This is the hardest example for me to translate, and I would like to hear a little bit more about it.

O'DONNELL: I'll see if I can. Actually, we are not quite sure how we are going to handle this. We may not release this program at all, because it is a matter of employee relations at duPont. Nevertheless, we can talk about generalities.

We feel that we have good identification of the behavior of the competent supervisor in a situation such as a contact with one of his men in which the man is upset. We do not use case studies, incidentally. They might sound like case studies, but they are not. We make it more specific. We will use conversation, comments, quotations that you said this and he said that, what behavior you observed, and other specific factors. I think possibly Dr. Skinner's book on analysis of behavior will solve a lot of our probems, but we have not used this. We are really trying to teach these men to recognize aspects of behavior in themselves, as well as in their employees. In recognizing them, they can then monitor themselves as they go about their daily work, after they leave the teaching machine or programed text. The real difficulty is perhaps in being precise, getting your stimulus-response pattern down to what you want. As you say, it is easier to draw a sketch or put down a rule. This is pretty easy. It is quite a bit more difficult to be that precise in language.

PETER: It sounds as if you are describing terminal behavior in different words than you have previously used. This is trying to give the trainee some diagnostic skills by exposing him to different kinds of responses so he has to look at the reasons for this kind of expression, a sort of sensitivity training.

Comment: I have a general comment here. I have been impressed with all three papers. One thing that impressed me most was the fact that in each of these three companies, the programs were developed by personnel within the organization, people who had been temporarily or permanently assigned to the project. I am wondering whether there is anyone here who may have some comment on this, as compared with experience in utilizing outside consultants.

BRUCE: Well, Bell Laboratories has used outside consultants.

HOLT: We employed Mike Woolman who was then with HumRRO as our man with programing expertise, and the subject matter expert was a company man.

McNamara: In other words, you had a combined situation here, one man within the company and one man out of it. I think there have been some experiences where companies have had somebody outside do the whole job and furnish the consultant with basic material. Bob, were you in on the program that Prudential Insurance Co. had produced for their salesman? Was that your outfit, or was that another one?

Glaser: No. AIR (American Institute for Research), under the direct supervision of Klaus, Shettel, and Clapp, built a life insurance program presenting the basic fundamentals of life insurance for LIAMA (Life Insurance Agency Management Association). What they did was to have a life insurance subject matter expert live at the AIR installation. It must have been for a period of eight weeks or so, not all at one time, but it was a long period.

Holt: Let's add that AIR has also had a chief operator from one of the telephone companies working at AIR for two years. This is a case in which AIR has a contract not specifically to develop programs, but to come up with a new training course, which is about 55% programed, as it turns out. The relationship is extremely close. We essentially furnish one person to them to work on this project. Other people have also worked very closely with the AIR people.

Hughes: I guess our experience falls somewhere between these others. We got into programed instruction at IBM about two years ago by calling on the services of Bob

Glaser and Dave Klaus. They started us off by helping to train our program writers, and then Dave Klaus helped us to review the programs each month as they were developed.

MCNAMARA: Maybe this is going off in a different direction, but I would like to bring up the subject of prepared programs, such as Tutortexts and things of this sort. In a couple of our IBM locations we have used Tutortexts in two subjects. One was on arithmetic for computers, and the other was on electronics. In one location they said that one of the books was wonderful and the other one was not very good; in another location it was exactly the opposite. These were two setups where one did not actually know what the other was doing, and I got independent reports from them. One said one thing and the other said another thing. From some of the general comments, I concluded that the experience in the two locations was dependent primarily on the trainees that studied the texts. In one location the classes were appropriate for one and not for the other. In the other location, it was just reversed. The nature of the training population can therefore very greatly influence the evaluation of these materials. I wonder if anybody else has had experience with commercially available programs.

O'DONNELL: We also have used purchased programs. In fact, we would prefer to do this. Even though we may be productive at it, we suspect that it would be more economical to buy them than to produce them. We have used some commercially produced programs when they fit a particular situation. We found them quite effective.

BRUCE: We have used purchased programs, and I agree with Larry that buying what somebody else has prepared is a much less expensive way of getting material. But let me give you an example of our big problem. We have a course in statistics that has been in operation for almost four years. We have used the TMI statistical course. The people who are teaching our course are very unhappy with the section on analysis of variance in the TMI program. They feel that it does not do the job. What I would like them to do is to program their own material in this area, but they are comfortable teaching it by the conventional blackboard-homework-assigned reading method, and they are continuing to do it.

O'DONNELL: May I interrupt you there? You say that these instructors who are using the statistics program do not assign all of it? They delete some of it and trainees go through the rest of it, and that part that is missing the instructors teach by the regular conventional method?

BRUCE: That's right. They have done the same thing for the TMI program on statistical inference. They are actually just using two of the ten chapters on statistical inference as assigned reading. Trainees read that and report to class.

Question: What do you think of the possibility of telling TMI to revise their book?

McNAMARA: I think you have the same situation here as we do with textbooks. There probably is not an instructor

IV

SOME ASPECTS OF

IBM RESEARCH ON PROGRAMED

INSTRUCTION *

J . L . H U G H E S [†]

For various reasons, I would like to keep my remarks informal so that you will ask some questions as I present my material. One reason is that I think we have a small enough group to make this kind of approach possible. The second reason is my commitment to programed instruction and the stimulus-response sequence. I have found that I begin to have guilt feelings if I go on speaking for too long a period of time without getting any responses from

* Portions of this chapter were published previously in the American Management Association Management Report No. 72, *Revolution in Training*, 1962; *Journal of Programed Instruction*, Vol. I, No. 1, 1962; *Training Directors Journal*, July 1962; *Applied Programed Instruction* by Margulies and Eigen, 1962; and the *Journal of Applied Psychology*, 1961, 45, pp. 225-231. We wish to thank the American Management Association, the Journal of Programed Instruction, the American Society of Training Directors, John Wiley and Sons, Inc., and the American Psychological Association, respectively, for permission to reprint them here.

† Consultant, Education Research, International Business Machines Corp.

the audience. So if you cooperate by making a few responses to reassure me, I will do my best to reinforce them positively.

Like others at this meeting, we would like to pay homage to Dr. B. F. Skinner and those classes of Harvard undergraduates who first demonstrated the effectiveness of programed instruction as an instructional method. Mainly as a result of Dr. Skinner's writings, our Applied Personnel Research staff began in 1959 to consider seriously the possibility of using programed instruction as an industrial training method for our employees and customers. As some of you may know from first hand experience, we do a great amount of training because of the nature of our equipment. As a result of the increasing rate of technological improvement and the introduction of new products, these training needs are increasing rapidly. For this reason, we are very interested in any new methods of instruction which promise to make our training procedures more efficient. However, we are confronted with a bit of a problem. Our training executives are very practical people, and they look askance at results based merely on Harvard sophomores. To appreciate this position, you must remember that in 1959 programed instruction was still a largely untried method which was unknown outside a small circle of psychologists. As a result, we had to conduct our own studies to answer the inevitable question, "Will this new method work in IBM?" For this reason—and also out of plain curiosity— we proposed an exploratory research project early in 1960 to investigate the feasibility of programed instruction for company training.

OBJECTIVES OF STUDY

The aims of this exploratory project were as follows: We wanted to study the problems involved in selecting and training company personnel as program writers. We wanted to study the problems involved in preparing, editing and testing programs. We wanted to find out the rate at which programs could be written in our company, and their cost, because, back in 1959, there were no data available on these important practical considerations. There was also the important matter of determining the kinds of courses for which programed instruction was most suited.

We manufacture different kinds of equipment, including electronic computers, electro-mechanical accounting machines and electric typewriters. We train many different types of our own personnel—salesmen, computer systems people, computer maintenance engineers, machine operators, and technical, engineering, manufacturing, supervisory, and management personnel, in addition to customer personnel. Therefore we have a wide range of subjects and people to be taught, and it was important for us to determine the characteristics of those courses which lend themselves most readily to programed instruction.

Another prime purpose of the project was to provide objective data with which to evaluate the relative effectiveness of programed instruction and conventional instruction. To do this, we adopted three criteria: classroom presentation time, learning achievement, and trainee attitude. Our reasoning was that a demonstration of reduction in classroom time would suggest certain economies resulting in a lower company training budget. An improvement in learning achievement would indicate the potential of programed instruction in developing better-trained personnel and customers. Finally, satisfactory trainee attitude toward programed instruction would indicate that the trainees would accept this new technique and offer no opposition to its further development. Obviously, even though you have a successful new teaching technique, it would not be very feasible as a training method in industry if it caused too much rebellion among employees and customers. If these initial studies were completed successfully, we contemplated carrying out more theoretical studies in an attempt to isolate and manipulate the significant variables associated with programed instruction in order to understand more about this technique and improve its efficiency in training programs.

DESCRIPTION OF STUDY

Walt McNamara and I, as members of the Applied Personnel Research group on the Corporate Staff, therefore made a research proposal in January, 1960, to the representatives of our operating divisions. These are the people who actually manufacture and market our products. Our proposal was that there was a new training technique which offered tremendous potential for industrial training. If they would provide skilled personnel who understood the technical requirements of our machines, we would teach these men the principles of programing, review the programs written, and carry out studies to evaluate their effectiveness.

As a result of this meeting, several program writers from two separate divisions were assigned to the project. We began the training program in March 1960. In this work we were greatly helped by Bob Glaser and Dave Klaus from the University of Pittsburgh and the American Institute for Research, respectively. Dave Klaus remained with us, coming in each month to help me review the programs written by the three program writers. These programs were designed for the training of equipment maintenance engineering personnel on the following three machines: the 7070 Data Processing System, the SAGE computer, and the 083 Sorter.* I would like to describe a series of studies completed on one of these programs, the one on the 7070 Data Processing System.

By September, 1960, five programed textbooks containing 719 frames were completed. (Incidentally, writing on this program was continued later so that the program now totals over 1,300 frames.) The program was of the linear, constructed-response variety and covered the first fifteen hours of conventional classroom presentation in a sixteen-week course. This amount of class time would be

---

* The program writers participating in the project were L. R. O'Neal (7070), J. Baker (083), Data Processing Division, and H. Yochman (SAGE) Federal Systems Division.

equivalent to five weeks of a three-hour college course. The topics included were the names and functions of units of the 7070 system, bit coding, data flow, characteristics of data and instruction words, and the program step. To test the effectiveness of programed instruction for teaching this kind of material, the following study was designed:

EXPERIMENTAL DESIGN

Two classes totaling 42 trainees who reported to the training center during September, 1960, were designated the control classes. Such trainees are generally graduates of technical schools, although many of them also have some college training or a degree. Their mental ability compares favorably with college graduates. They are usually men in their late 20's who, after several years' experience servicing our basic unit record equipment, have been selected for advanced training on computers.

The control classes were taught the introductory material of the course by two different experienced instructors using the conventional classroom method (lecture-discussion). This instruction covered a period of four mornings and totaled fifteen hours, three hours on the first morning and four hours on each of the remaining three mornings. The afternoons of each day were spent on another phase of 7070 training. On the fifth morning, these classes were administered a comprehensive two-hour achievement test consisting of 88 completion and multiple-choice items. This test was prepared by the program writing team with the cooperation of several training center instructors. A new test was necessary because no satisfactory objective test of sufficient length was available for the part of the course taught by programed instruction.

Six classes containing a total of 70 trainees made up the initial experimental group. Two of these classes reported for training each month from October through December, 1960. They were instructed solely by means of programed textbooks, which were substituted for the lectures and discussions covering the introductory part of the course.

The control and experimental groups were run consecutively rather than concurrently in order to reduce any contamination of results. Since members of both classes starting each month at the training center might come from the same company field office and might also room together, it was decided to eliminate the possibility that study materials would be exchanged by control and experimental trainees during evening study periods.

The class instructors were directed to act as if the programed textbooks were part of the regular classroom procedure in order to minimize the Hawthorne effect. (As the months went by, the texts did become the standard procedure.) It was never mentioned to the students that they were participating in an experiment. The instructors confined their role to stating at the beginning of the first class period that this section of the course would be taught by five self-explanatory programed textbooks. They then passed out the first programed text. The third and fifth texts were passed out at the beginning of the second and third days of the experiment, respectively. The second and fourth texts were given to the trainees during the first and second classroom periods, respectively, after they had finished the texts passed out at the beginning of the period.

The classroom time allotted for programed texts was reduced to eleven hours spread over a three-day period, with three hours on the first day and four hours on each of the last two days. This reduction in classroom presentation time was based on fairly conservative estimates of the time needed for trainees to complete the programed texts during the instruction period. The reason for deliberately pacing the completion of the five programed texts over the three-day period in this manner was to assure better administrative control. This experimental design, however, prevented the faster students from finishing all of the texts before the third day, and did not permit the direct measurement of the full saving in presentation time possible under pro-gramed instruction.

After passing out the texts at the beginning of each class period, the instructors retired to the back of the class-room and confined their activities to recording the number of frames that each trainee completed in class. They were also instructed to answer as briefly as possible the questions asked by trainees. A record was kept of all questions asked.

The experimental classes also took the same compre-hensive achievement test on the day following the comple-tion of their instruction. In addition, they anonymously completed a questionnaire asking them to evaluate programed instruction. The questionnaire consisted of five items with five-point descriptive scales measuring the effectiveness, difficulty, and acceptability of programed instruction, and three open-end questions asking for any general comments and any aspects of programed instruction particularly liked or disliked.

To avoid interference with the administration of the company training center, no attempt was made to assign trainees to class by random procedures. Instead, men were assigned to classes in the customary manner as they were reported available for training by their office managers in the field. In planning the experiment, it was anticipated that analysis of covariance procedures would make it possible to control background variables which differed for the control and experimental groups and which were correlated with achievement test scores.

To test the comparability of the control and experimental groups on various background data, such as age, educational level, total months of experience, and previous computer experience, data were collected by means of an education and experience questionnaire. A company-developed test of reasoning ability (Programer Aptitude Test) was also administered. The significance of differences on these variables for the control and experimental groups and the correlations of these variables with achievement test scores were calculated.

BRUCE: You arbitrarily cut four hours off the time?

HUGHES: Yes. From our trials of the program, we estimated how long it would take the average trainee to complete it. We decided that if we reduced the classroom presentation time to eleven hours, the trainee would have no difficulties in covering this material. The four-hour reduction was also sufficient to demonstrate to management a significant decrease in classroom training time. Of course, we had no control over what these trainees did at home, because we gave them the programed instruction material to take home for study. We were not optimistic enough to believe that we could get reliable estimates from the trainees of the time they spent on home study. In the attitude questionnaire, however, we did ask them whether they had spent more or less time on programed instruction than on conventional instruction. Only 16% replied that programed instruction required more home study.

DEESE: They did have the programed instruction to take home?

HUGHES: Yes. Our reasoning was that in the normal training situation, they have the training materials to take home to study. In any future use of this course in the company, they would also have the material to take home to study. Therefore, we wanted to simulate the usual conditions as much as we could.

This completes my description of the experimental design. Before I present the results, does anyone have any other questions?

BECK: How do you justify the limiting of time by pacing the trainees when the whole idea of programing is to allow the student to progress at his own speed?

HUGHES: We left a very comfortable period of time for the students to complete the program. Within these limits, however, they had to adjust to their own individual pace. I think, as a practical matter, it is important to impose some kind of pacing on people. We have found, as Ollie (Holt) and others have, that there are wide discrepancies in the time trainees take to complete programed material if they are not paced in some way. Those of you who have had some experience in administering psychological tests know that if you give a test to a group of people, you generally find out that if most people can finish in an hour, for example, practically all the rest will finish in the next half-hour. However, one or two people will take an additional 2 hours if you give them that much time. So you have to impose some kind of time limit to make trainees aware of the fact that they should be working fairly rapidly.

HOLT: Did these trainees have laboratory exercises?

HUGHES: No. These men studied the programed material in the morning, and in the afternoon they studied other material on circuits.

CHLDS: John, in cutting down the classroom time from fifteen to eleven hours, did you give the program to enough people prior to establishing an eleven-hour time limit?

HUGHES: We gave it to about a half dozen. The results made us feel that eleven hours was a comfortable period of time.

RESULTS

HUGHES: The first result concerns classroom presentation time. The experimental classes easily covered the programed instruction material within the allotted eleven hours of classroom time, thereby saving 27% in classroom presentation time. We also kept records on the individual completion times of those units of the program studied in class. From these estimates, we arrived at an average estimated completion time for the entire program of 9.8 hours and a standard deviation of 1.8 hours. The range was from 7.2 hours to 15.3 hours. Despite the pacing, there was a considerable range of completion times.

CHILDS: You told them that they would have to complete the program in eleven hours, but some of them obviously did not. Did they know if they would be given additional time if the eleven-hour time limit was up?

HUGHES: No, they were told that they would have eleven hours to study this material in class. It was up to them to cover the rest of the material at home.

The second result pertained to learning achievement. In checking the background data for the control and experimental classes, we found that the experimental classes were significantly higher (.01 level) on one of these variables, the Programer Aptitude Test (the mental ability test). They averaged 58.2 as compared to 51.2 for the control group. After running an analysis of covariance to partial out the effect of this difference in initial mental ability scores, we found there was a significant difference in achievement (.01 level) between the experimental class and the control classes. The adjusted scores of the experimental classes on the achievement test averaged 94.7 compared to 86.9 for the control classes. These test scores were expressed as the percent of items correct because of our desire to facilitate communication with our company executives who tend to think in terms of a test score based on 100%.

We also found a considerable reduction in the range of scores for our experimental classes. The experimental classes had a standard deviation of 3.8, and the control classes had a standard deviation of 7.0. The difference was significant at the .02 level. This finding is consistent with a number of other results indicating a restriction of range as a result of using programed instruction. Thus, this study demonstrated that programed instruction can result in higher achievement and greater homogeneity of achievement for a group of our computer service engineering trainees.*

O'DONNELL: What was the minimum score on the exam?

HUGHES: One way of answering your question would be to consider the percentage of trainees at various score

---

* For a more complete statistical treatment of these results, see Hughes, J. L., and McNamara, W. J., "A Comparative Study of Programed and Conventional Instruction in Industry," *J. Applied Psychol.*, 1961, 45, 225-231.

levels. The minimum score on the experimental group was somewhere between 80 and 84, while the minimum score on the control group was between 65 and 69. Only 11% of the experiment group scored below 90 on this test compared to 55% for the control group. In evaluating these results, it is also important to consider the general level of achievement test scores at the training center before the study began. The average for a successful class was somewhere between 80 and 85. It looks therefore as if one could argue that the achievement of the control classes was certainly typical of the results obtained previously with lecture-discussion presentations.

BRUCE: What was the length of time between completing the course and taking the test?

HUGHES: The test was given to all classes on the next day.

DEESE: Was this an objective test?

HUGHES: Yes, the test consisted of multiple-choice and short completion items.

SEIDEL: Do you feel that there was an advantage in having the experimental group complete the material in eleven hours? Would it have been possible to have the control group complete it in eleven hours?

HUGHES: This course had been given for some time at the training center and had been subjected to a number of reductions in classoom time. At the time of the study, it was presumably down to the minimum time considered necessary by the training administrators at the center. This was certainly true in the opinion of the instructors giving the course.

Question: Would you tell us what the highest score was in the control group?

HUGHES: I don't recall what the top score was, but there were five men out of the 42 in the control group who had scores of 95 and above.

Question: I have seen some programs that give clues to the responses, such as the first letter of a word or syllables. How do you feel about this?

HUGHES: My feeling is that cues of this kind should be minimized. There is some evidence—the study of Sue Meyer (Markle), for example—which indicates that this type of cue is helpful with children. With adults, however, I think this kind of cue should be minimized, because you can use it too much and speckle your program with the initial letters of responses and underscores rather than using semantic or linguistic cues to obtain the desired responses. But this is a matter for experimentation. We don't really know the value of these things.

The third variable measured was trainee attitude toward programed instruction. On the questionnaire administered anonymously to the six experimental classes, the replies of the trainees were very favorable. Of the total group of 70 men, 87% like programed instruction more than conventional instruction, and 83% said they would prefer using it in future IBM courses. Only 6% liked programed instruction less than conventional instruction, and 13% would have some objections to using it in future courses. A possible reason for the size of the latter negative response was the impression of some students that programed instruction would replace the use of instructors and class discussions completely in future courses.

The questionnaire also provided the trainees with several open-end questions asking what they particularly liked or disliked about programed instruction. In their responses, 69 of the 70 trainees mentioned some aspect which they liked. A content analysis indicated that the most frequently liked aspects were its effectiveness as an instruction method (46 comments); certain characteristics of the method itself, such as the repetition of important points, the gradual and logical sequence of presentation, the way it maintained the student's attention and concentration (23 comments); and the ability to proceed at one's own rate (10 comments). It appeared from these comments that, through their own experience with programed instruction, the trainees themselves recognized a number of the advantages usually ascribed to it.

In response to the question on what they particularly disliked, 40 of the 70 trainees wrote in a number of comments, but no single comment was made by many individuals. For example, there was criticism of the need to turn pages constantly (8 comments), the amount of repetition and the number of written responses required (6 comments), the amount of time allotted for studying the materials (7 comments), and the absence of an instructor and class discussion (5 comments). Another criticism made by seven trainees was the failure of the programed text used in this study to provide adequate summaries or outlines of the topics covered to aid in reviewing the material.

From these results, it appeared that trainee attitude was favorable and there were no serious objections to programed instruction as an industrial training method. However, a number of negative comments had been made regarding some features of the programed texts, and further studies therefore were designed to modify the features of these texts in order to remove these criticisms and possibly improve the efficiency of the texts. The programed texts in the original study were in the horizontal format. This had its origin in an attempt to simulate a Skinner teaching machine. A frame was presented in the top panel of a page, and the trainee turned to the top panel of the next page for the correct answer. He then turned to the succeeding page for the next frame, and so on. We have now come to recognize that this format is not very efficient. Back in early 1960, however, we used it because it had been successfully employed in the Pittsburgh high school physics study by Klaus and Lumsdaine, and we wanted to see if these results could be replicated in an industrial study. Later on, as we worked with this format, we realized that a number of changes could be made.

DESCRIPTION OF SECOND STUDY

The purpose of the next study to be reported was therefore to measure the effect of changes in programed text
format and a further reduction in classroom presentation
time on learning achievement and attitude. The changes in
the programed texts were designed to make them more
efficient for use in industrial training. Since these changes
took place during a six-month period, an opportunity was
also provided to observe the effect of using programed instruction over an extended period of time.

EXPERIMENTAL DESIGN

The six classes totaling 70 men who were trained with
the original programed text format from October through
December, 1960, became the control group in this study.
Nine classes totaling 129 men who reported to the company
training center for 7070 training during the period from
January through June, 1961, constituted the experimental
groups. Except for test format changes and reduction of
classroom time, the experimental procedure remained the
same. The experimental classes were subjected to the following four different experimental conditions:

I. For two classes reporting in January, classroom time was reduced to eight hours (four hours a day for two days) from the eleven hours (three hours the first day, four hours the last two days) taken by the control classes. This was a significant reduction because in addition to losing hours of classroom time, the trainee lost one evening for home study. (Remember that the average program completion time in the first study had been 9.8 hours, with a standard deviation of 1.8 hours). The programed text format was not changed.

II. For two February classes, classroom time was maintained at eight hours, but was spread over a period of three days instead of two in order to ease the pressure on the trainees. Trainees wrote their answers on separate answer pads instead of in the texts (as in the control classes). This change would permit the programed texts to be used repeatedly and reduce the number of texts needed. Since the trainee could now see all of his previous answers before him on the answer pad, we were interested in the possible effect this chance for "cheating" might have on achievement.

III. For three March and April classes, classroom time was unchanged. Trainees continued to write their answers on answer pads. Correct answers to frames were printed on the backs of pages in the texts instead of on the following pages (as in the control classes). This change was designed to reduce page turning by 50%, thereby possibly saving time and eliminating a minor source of trainee dissatisfaction.

IV. For two May and June classes, classroom

time remained the same, and the answers to frames were printed on the back of pages as before. Trainees continued to write answers on answer pads but wrote them for only 17% of the frames. Thus, most of the overt responding was eliminated.

The effect of these four changes in experimental conditions was studied using the achievement test and the questionnaire described previously as well as unit completion time records maintained by instructors in class. Now let us briefly consider the results.*

There were no significant differences in learning achievement among the control and experimental classes. The mean achievement test scores ranged from 93.7 to 95.3, with standard deviations of 3.3 to 6.8. Learning achievement thus continued to hold up in the experimental classes, regardless of changes in the programed text format and classroom presentation time. These findings suggest that programed instruction is a more hardy specimen than we suspected in the beginning and that many of the rituals originally insisted on may not be necessary.

Incidentally, for all the classes taught by programed instruction, learning achievement continued to be significantly higher than that attained by conventionally taught classes (a mean of 86.9, standard deviation of 7.0). Although classroom presentation time thus was reduced from

* For a fuller presentation of these results, See Hughes, J. L., *Effect of Changes in Programed Text Format and Reduction in Classroom Time on the Achievement and Attitude of Industrial Trainees, J. Progr. Inst.*, Vol. 1, No. 1, 1962.

eleven hours in the control classes to eight hours in the experimental classes, there was no decrease in learning achievement. Since conventional instruction (lecture-discussion) had originally required fifteen hours to present this material, the total reduction in classroom presentation time was 47%.

BRUCE: When you changed the format, did you cut out all except 17% of the overt responses?

HUGHES: Yes, all of the strictly verbal responses were eliminated in the last experimental condition.

COOK: How was that 17% distributed?

HUGHES: In various ways, depending on the unit of the program. In the first unit, the overt response frames were toward the end of the unit. In the other units, they were scattered throughout. The criteria was to retain all the responses that required drawings, diagrams, coding and computations. All of the purely verbal responses were eliminated.

You will recall that we also collected data on the time taken by trainees to complete units of the program in class, in order to determine the effect of changes in text format. Experimental Condition IV (covert responding) was the only one to produce a significant difference, a reduction of approximately 20%.

The reduction in classroom presentation time from eleven to eight hours in the experimental classes put more pressure on the trainees to work faster in class. It also caused more of them to spend additional time on home study. They also believed that future programed instruction classes would continue to exclude interaction with an instructor. From their comments on the student questionnaire, it appeared that these factors increased their negative reaction to programed instruction. However, it did not reach a high level. For example, 19% liked programed instruction less than conventional instruction, and 33% objected to using it in future classes. These percents compared to 6% and 13%, respectively, for the control classes.

It was also demonstrated that a further reduction in classroom presentation time up to 47% was possible under programed instruction. This reduction, however, was accomplished only at the cost of increased student dissatisfaction with programed instruction. Although student dissatisfaction did not become very strong, these findings underlined the importance of carefully planning the introduction of programed instruction into industrial training, and of providing for conditions which maintained the desired level of student satisfaction.

McNamara: I think you might comment more on the effect of the reduction of classroom time to eight hours (four hours a day for two days) in the first experimental condition.

Hughes: As I mentioned before, there was no effect on learning achievement. As might be expected, however, the trainee's attitude toward programed instruction became more negative. For example, 6% of the control group said they liked conventional instruction better than programed instruction. For the first experimental condition, the figure was 14%, more than double.

Question: Was the actual amount of time they took to complete the program about the same?

HUGHES: The amount of time for the first experimental group, as estimated from records kept by instructors in class, was not significantly different from that of the control classes. It appeared that the latter classes had originally paced themselves to work pretty much at their maximum speed. This is understandable because they were a highly motivated group trying to learn a new subject. Incidentally, the first experimental group made up for the reduction in classroom time by spending more time on homework. On the questionnaire, 54% said that there was more home study with programed than conventional instruction, compared to only 16% for the control classes. The increased requirement for home study undoubtedly was a cause of their greater negative reaction to programed instruction. In order to control trainee attitude, therefore, the number of classroom days was increased from two to three with later experimental classes, thereby providing an additional evening for home study.

DEESE: Did they have programed material available to them for homework?

HUGHES: Yes. We merely added the programed texts to the conventional material they already had, such as a manual and a study guide.

Deese: Was there any indication that the group that was forced at this higher rate used the conventional material?

Hughes: I have no direct evidence on that. I would suspect that trainees had their hands full studying the programed texts, particularly the slower trainees.

Childs: You said that you started out with programed texts in the ribbon (horizontal) format and then made various modifications. Did you ever get around to a vertical format or did you deliberately avoid it?

Hughes: We were quite interested in doing that, but at the time, the support needed to do the extensive typing and reproduction job was not available. It was easy to make the kind of changes we did. They required only minor adjustments in reproduction. To go to a vertical from a horizontal format, however, requires complete re-typing and reproduction of the program.

To conclude, our studies indicated that programed instruction did not lose its effectiveness when used by succeeding classes totaling 199 trainees at a company training center over a period of nine months. The findings also showed that changes improving the efficiency of the original horizontal programed text format were possible without reducing learning achievement. Greater flexibility in the design of programed texts therefore appears to be a fruitful subject for future investigation.

The other conclusion relates to trainee attitude. In our studies, reducing classroom time by 27% to 47% of the original class lecture period resulted in a sacrifice of some trainee satisfaction with programed instruction. The level of dissatisfaction fortunately remained low. These findings underline the need for planning and care in the introduction of programed instruction in industrial training. Reasonable periods of time should be allocated for study, for example, rather than trying to save too much time initially and putting heavy pressure on trainees to proceed quickly. Otherwise, it is possible for trainee dissatisfaction to interfere with the gains in learning achievement and reductions in training time possible with programed instruction.

DISCUSSION

DR. ROBERT GLASER: Just a couple of preliminary remarks before I talk about the paper. It just impressed me last night that John Glenn is going to have to do it all over again, because he did not have a control group. The other point is that I believe that this conference has broken through the data barrier. I know many of you, and I particularly, have squirmed through many conferences on programed learning where the bulk of the talk was on promises, aspirations, and the differences between big and small steps. It is delightful to hear some evidence and data presented.

Returning to the previous paper, I am impressed with the fact that they had trouble getting subjects, because you need subjects at your side all the time. I suspect there may be a new occupation called "professional subject." This is not so far from wrong. I think Don Cook told me that they have full time learners on whom programs are tried out. It is not a bad idea.

I'm very impressed with John's attempt to push the pacing. I think this has both applied and theoretical ramifications in regard to the extent to which students can be paced. While we say that each subject can go at his

186

own pace, I think it would be interesting to test the limits of pacing. I guess Bob Gagne and Jim Deese know more about this than I do. There have been some studies, mostly in England, on the effect of pacing and timing and so forth. Pacing is an interesting variable to investigate, and I think it might result in some interesting gains.

I was going over an early version of John's paper, and I noticed that his people completed about one hundred frames an hour, and Larry's people also completed about one hundred frames an hour in completing their programs. It seems to me that reading one hundred frames an hour appears to be a reasonable rate for the kinds of frames that you people have written. Students seem to be able to read that many. I don't know what your experience has been, Jim.

BRUCE: Our mean was 115 frames, and our average time was sixty minutes.

HUGHES: Actually, Bob, we had 719 frames in our 7070 program, and the average speed of completion was slightly less than ten hours. That would put us down to about seventy to seventy-five frames an hour.

DEESE: Is there any data on readability of frames, aside from the responding factor?

GLASER: Aside from the fact that students get the right answer, can some frames be easier to read? No, I don't know of any data.

BRUCE: In the sensitometry program, you cannot do this because there are a lot of calculations. When you have calculations in a frame, this will stretch your time.

HOLT: There was the same sort of thing in our program. I think that our mean was about fifty frames an hour, but some of the frames took as much as ten minutes to answer and work the problem.

GLASER: There is an interesting point on frames in which you have to work a problem. It has been my experience with mathematics frames in which students have to solve problems that the act of solving the problem is very reinforcing. The students often know when they get a problem right, and they often ignore the necessity for looking at the right answer as a reinforcement. You set up the problem so well that they work through it. It's very reinforcing to be able to do all these operations that they may not have done before, and this serves as a reinforcement in itself. Sometimes they hardly look at the answer. I am impressed that you can leave out, especially in low error rate programs, a lot of the information feedback for many frames, because performing is reinforcing in itself, and the information feedback is often ignored by the students. Sometimes it is necessary to force them to look at it, but that has some instrumentation problems.

I like the idea of casting your scores in terms of 100%, because to my way of thinking, you are saying on the final examination that all the questions are what I really want the program to teach. The extent to which you fall below 100% gives you a mark by which to improve your program, and I think that is a good way to look at it.

The reduction in variability which keeps coming up in all of the papers has an interesting aspect. The reduction that you get with a programed group is not a reduction on both ends of the distribution. What happens is that you usually block out the poor scores. The good people in both groups appear to do well. The good people in conventional situations apparently have developed ways of learning that are very efficient. In programed learning, we are trying to find out what these are and give them to other students. The reduction in heterogeneity seems to happen this way; you pull up the people at the lower end of the conventional distribution and do not affect the others too much. This may be due to the fact that at the present stage of programing, we do not do well enough at improving the already efficient habits of the good students.

Comment: There is another reason, and that is that the tests have a ceiling. The next step is harder tests.

GLASER: That's right. If the scores are close to 100, then you have a ceiling.

Comment: You could make the tests harder.

GAGNE: No. Just test what you are trying to test—neither hard nor easy—just test.

HUGHES: I think that is exactly the point. We are not in the business of making hard tests. We are trying to set up criteria to measure the achievement of the course objectives. If students meet these criteria, that is fine.

GLASER: That is right. That is related to the point that a good test is one that gives you maximum discrimination among people. That is, of course, only true for aptitude tests, where you are trying to maximize your validity coefficients. In proficiency tests, I suspect that frequently the best thing that could happen is that everybody would get the same high score. I guess that is the point that Bob Gagne is making. The point I am trying to make is that the reduction in heterogeneity has this effect. It is not pulling everybody down to a mean score or an average score or something like this. Instead, you drop out the poorer performers.

Another thing that concerns me is that in most studies where we compare two groups, we have a difference of six, eight or nine points that is statistically significant. I don't know exactly what eight or nine points mean practically to you people in industry. Nine points more on a test, what does it mean? Is it more than a statistically significant difference on the test? Is it something you would consider a real achievement? That's why I feel the need for saying something more about achievement than just an improvement of eight or nine points. We need to say something about what the eight or nine points mean in terms of the competence of the group, in terms of what they can do.

GAGNE: Do you feel that one kind of statistic mentioned in John Hughes' report is perhaps more meaningful? He said, as I remember it, that in the experimental group, a very small per cent (11%) scored below 90 on the achievement test, whereas in the other group, 55% scored below 90. This of course reflects the same point made by Bob Glaser. I would think that this is a very meaningful kind of statistic.

DEESE: There is another question. It concerns whether the test itself is in any sense an ultimate criterion. It may be that an eight or nine point difference, or 55% getting above 90 as opposed to 11%, is important or is a big difference on a test. But is the test itself an ultimate criterion? And is there any way of looking for more ultimate criteria?

GLASER: Well, the point is, what does 55% mean? I feel that 55% means that these students can do something on the computer or do something in sensitometry.

GAGNE: Now you are talking Jim Deese's language.

GLASER: I suspect your language, too, in the sense of the meaningfulness of 55% in terms of some behavioral statement of what they can do.

DEESE: You see it may be that those few items which represent the small difference between the experimental and control groups are very critical with respect to performance on the job. This may be the difference between a fellow who is really good at maintenance engineering and one who is not. But, of course, you don't know. It may be a difference that is completely unimportant on the actual job.

Comment: This is one of the hardest things to measure, of course, the transfer of what you teach a class to the actual performance on the job, especially when you are after retention building. We ran into this with industrial engineers who had taken the statistics course, both lecture and others. Some of them went out and were given assignments where they had to use statistics. They went back and re-studied it and then used it. When we tested these people, they were way up at 100%. We had other people who were given assignments which required no statistics at all. At a given period, they had dropped way off in their knowledge. I think one reason we probably go to test data in comparing is that it is easily available right after the training. It is what happens in the interim that we have no control over.

GLASER: I would like to ask another question, John. Comparing the length of time usually taken for your course as base line data with the number of hours taken to read the frames, could you say from your paper that you obtained about a 50% savings in time?

HUGHES: The classroom presentation time was reduced by as much as 47%. I would say the optimum saving would probably be somewhere between the 27% saved in the first studies and the 47% saved in later studies. That's a conservative figure.

GLASER: I guess the other point to be made is that John's shifting around with the response modes from covert to overt responding is very useful. We don't know much, I suspect, about the extent to which we can get away with certain modes of responding, and how well they transfer to other modes of responding. If one mode of responding is more efficient and less time consuming, it is certainly worth trying it out and seeing to what extent it is transferable. It seems to me from some of the things I see happening in programing, that the transfer in some areas of knowledge, the transfer between knowing it verbally and being able to do it nonverbally, is very high, and in other areas it may be less so. I think it is a matter for your own experimentation to see how much you can get away with in not requiring elaborate responses and the appropriate instrumentation that goes with them.

BRUCE: In a comparison of overt vs. covert responses, does anyone have any data on the retention that a person would have with information in relation to the way he responded? It would seem to me that if the person did not construct the response, did not write it down, his retention would be a lot less than if he did.

DEESE: This is a very good question, because as I have seen the data in programed instruction, it has tended to go towards the direction that the use of overt and covert responses does not make any difference. But this is, as near as I can determine, on the basis of an immediate test. I think that there are some theoretical reasons from the data available in other fields in experimental psychology for suggesting that there may be some difference between covert and overt responding if you have a retention interval, if you have a period in which this material is not activated. One reason is the very one which enables you to cut down the program time, namely, the rate at which this material is worked on. Secondly, and this depends a little on the nature of the individual items, I think that it is easy for someone who is responding in a covert way to respond partially, that is, to respond to some part of the material. I think I can illustrate this. Suppose you have frame one which requires a certain response and then frame two requiring a response which is in part determined by the contents of the preceeding frame. If the student does not respond completely to the first item, but says, "Oh, that's x," and then goes on immediately to the next one, the next time this bit of information is called for, he does not have this context between items one and two. The result is that the second response has not been completely made to the material which is relevant in this item. I think in achievement tests the context of the entire course material is more neatly organized. Over a longer period of time, however, these kinds of relations may fall apart so that the response you want the student to produce has been forgotten. The material is more easily forgotten if a response has not been overtly and directly made to it. There are data which suggest that there should be a difference in retention depending on whether the response is overt or covert, and I have always been a little puzzled by the data on programed learning that shows that there is no difference.

McNAMARA: I think that some of the data we have from experimental psychology indicates that the retention rate over a period of time is less because you don't have any reinforcement in between. In a good many situations, such as in 7070 training, the material learned is being reinforced. This is the reason that we did not collect retention data over a six-months period of time. In the ensuing weeks, these trainees are using this material, maybe not continually, but to quite a degree.

DEESE: That is all right if you are using it in the right way, but there is another interpretation of the use of the material. You see, when you set up a program, the responses which you are asking people to produce are by and large already part of their repertoire. They know the words, they know the numbers, and they know the basic operation that you start out with. These things are used in other contexts, in other closely related material. The modern interpretation of the determination of the forgetting says that it is the use of these same materials in other contexts which is responsible for forgetting. While it may be true that you get intervening reinforcements which strengthen this material so that you don't have to worry about forgetting, it also seems to be possible that you may get intervening learning, or performance, or diversion which compete with older ways of doing things, particularly if you are trying to teach somebody some new operations for some new machinery. These conditions produce forgetting.

COOK: On the major question of retention, there is still not much data. I think one reason is that time must elapse before you can do a retention study. As far as I know, Jim Holland at Harvard did the first major retention study in this field, except for the very good one that was presented yesterday (Ed. note: Holt's study). The question still remains, though, whether or not there might be a strategy for selecting which responses must be overt and which must not. I think that there is a little bit of data which suggests that John Hughes' trick was the right one. The Center for Programmed Instruction did a study contrasting overt and covert responding using a program that we had prepared at Basic Systems on the diagnosis of myocardial infarction with the electrocardiogram. This has a lot of frames which are the more usual kind of verbal frames, but it also has frames which require the recognition and sketching of electrocardiograph records. The final exam was given on the basis of the experiment and item-analyzed into two classes of responses, the more purely verbal responses and those which were based on recognition and sketching of the pattern. There was an interaction effect in that the covert-overt difference was nil, or nearly so, for the verbal materials, but strong for those which required use of the diagram. This suggests one approach to a strategy for selecting items which must be responded to overtly.

There is also the possibility that a general strategy can be involved. Try and imagine a program in which a person responds covertly most of the time under the continual threat of being required to respond overtly according to an intermittent or unpredictable schedule. He therefore never knows until after he has made his covert response, whether or not, this time, he is going to be asked to lay it on the line. Now it is an interesting procedural problem to bring this about, but with the right kind of classroom practice, it can be done, say where the teacher intermittently requests writing and then can check on it. Or in the long run, a machine can be designed in which you look at a frame, press a ready button and then the machine tells you okay, this time you go on to the next frame, or in some instances, now you have to write this one out. I think that you could actually program a procedure for bringing covert responses up to full strength of readiness for emission and in that way circumvent the dangers of fragmentary responding. At the same time, you would get all the virtues of time saving and perhaps even go beyond that and generate a program in strong and clear thinking. This is a dream of mine, anyhow.

V

PROGRAMED

TRAINING: AN INDUSTRIAL TOOL

R . J . M O R S E *

The concluding speaker of a conference often has a rather difficult task of not repeating information and data presented in earlier talks. In the area of programed training, this seldom presents a problem because of the vast amount of research that is being conducted and the relative controversial nature of many of the ideas you hear about.

I consider my task here both as a challenge and a relief. It is a challenge of my ability to express clearly to you my firm beliefs concerning programed training in industry; it is a relief because no speaker follows on the agenda to challenge my ideas!

It is difficult to separate the problem of programer selection from the broader area of utilization of programed training methodology in industry, since selection can follow utilization, and has in General Telephone Company of Cali-

* Instructional Methods Administrator, General Telephone Company of California, Santa Monica, California.

fornia. Thus, I shall depart from the title of my talk as shown in the original program and cover three main areas.

First, I shall discuss what becomes a very real problem when an industry decides to explore programed training utilization and that is, how do you best introduce to top management both the concept and the utilization of programed training?

Second, I shall give you my conclusions regarding some of the problems we must face regarding the uses of programed training based on research we have conducted.

Third, I'll finally get to the assigned subject and that is how do you select and train instructional programers?

The first thought which comes to management's mind whenever training is discussed is "How much will this cost?" Certainly training costs money and I doubt whether anyone would dispute this, but is this a logical *first* question? Should not the need for training be the first thing to consider, or, before you even discuss the need, shouldn't you first determine the problem? It is very easy to say that all industrial problems are really training problems and far too often, this actually happens. The training director is an easy target for a management which does not see fit to consider a discrepancy on its own merits and to be certain of what the real problem is.

When training is in fact discovered to be the problem, do you ever look at it this way: "How much is *not* training costing your company?" Would your employees reach a higher rate of productivity faster if training were improved? How many union grievances could be avoided or settled at first level if your supervisory personnel were made fully knowledgeable about the contract through a training program? Could your turnover be reduced if your employees were more highly motivated based on good training?

This approach, the cost of *not* training, is often a real eye opener and the trigger which starts an investigation of programed training with top management support.

Our company is, to my knowledge, the only large (over 1 million telephones in service) telephone company which operates on a decentralized basis where each operating division is in effect an entity in itself handling most aspects of telephone operations on a local level. This works well and gives local management both the responsibility and the authority for most operations. It also encourages creativity in its fullest sense because action plans may be tried out according to the wishes of local management, and if one division is doing better than another, soon those not doing as well explore the action plan which is working elsewhere. This is internal competition in its healthiest form.

However, it would only result in a great duplication and triplication of effort if research on new instructional methodology was conducted on such a decentralized basis. As with everything new, there are a few people involved in programed training who are eager to make the most money in the least amount of time. If these people were to impress neophyte local managers with their proposals, we would soon have ten different projects operating throughout the company, each with something different in mind, and each headed by one individual who felt his way was best.

Programed training research and implementation must be centralized, at least initially, as should research on any new instructional method. This permits the formation of a specialized function where the positions are held by people who are expert in the area. In this manner, control rests in one place. The staff members of the team can perform as analysts, working with content experts in all phases of the company operation. Others on the team might be the instructional programers who work with the analysts and content experts. What we are really doing is developing a skill (analyst and instructional programer) and then utilizing this skill throughout the company. By so doing, this one central point can sense very effectively the pulse of the entire organization as to its training needs and problems, and then send the doctors to diagnose the trouble. As this develops, you would certainly expect to attract followers among the content experts in the divisions. Here is where the centralized aspect of this function would become broader. To have attracted a follower in the first place, he must have been sold on what you were preaching. He then becomes an ally and can perform a very effective service in the field by being close to the actual "doers" of the work. This is by no means "empire building"; it is to me the most effective way of handling this type of activity. It is working very well in our company, although I must admit we are only two months into this type of centralized activity on instructional methods research, and I hesitate in giving any concrete conclusions, even though I am convinced of our continued success.

results, with other studies and finally begin to think about preparing your materials in-plant.

I hope you can appreciate the importance of a proper organizational and functioning relationship between a group which is researching programed training for the *company,* and the rest of the company. Only when control rests with one *accepted* group can the implementation be accomplished most successfully. I emphasize the word accepted because, to repeat, it is of no avail to force the concept on anyone. It need not be forced if it is understood and tested by reliable research designs.

Next, my conclusions regarding uses of programed training and some cautions in conducting research.

The lack of common denominators becomes very evident to me when reading the research data written to date. By common denominators I mean that when trying to compare data, one cannot find comparable variables. In over 90% of all studies I have read, where a classroom instructional method was compared to a programed approach, it was impossible for me to equate the "classroom instructional methods." Words such as "standard lecture," "conventional class," "lecture method," "normal way of instructing," etc., have been used by researchers, and how is one to know what is meant by these terms? We cannot assume that they each mean the same thing. I asked one author of such a study what he meant by his term "standard class." It turned out that not only was it *not* a standard class but in fact was more like a programed lecture. In a study we conducted at

General Telephone, we compared a programed course with the same material taught in lecture fashion. The instructor in the lecture group taught the material in the same sequence as covered in the programed course. He also used lesson plans developed from the programed materials.

This was certainly a very highly structured lecture and hardly conventional. Our results showed no differences in learning between groups on either the post-test or the retention examination given six weeks later. The programed groups did learn in considerably less time, but I wonder if this would have been true if our instructor was told to teach as *rapidly* as he could and not take a predetermined amount of time. (Of course, we might then have seen significantly less learning in this group.)

Type of learning environment is not the only variable which needs specific defining in reported studies, but this is the most critical one in my opinion. The need for common denominators and accepted definitions of terms is critical and is something we must insist upon as soon a possible; otherwise we will have a lot of interesting research much of which cannot be compared.

Another problem is terminology. Words such as linear, intrinsic, branching, etc. which were defined several years ago, now take on new meanings. Initial meanings for much of our jargon no longer apply, and it is very confusing for someone reading the literature for the first time, as well as reading current articles on the subject by different authors, to understand the content because of varying definitions of the words. I am not saying that I feel it wrong for two people to disagree on the meaning of a term, but only that it is time we set up some nomenclature that means the same to everyone. For example, to me, a program where multiple choice responses are required but where you are always returned to the "main line" frame, is a linear program if the frames contain a small amount of information and where wrong responses are either not explained at all or only very briefly explained. I consider this to be a "thick" linear program instead of a "thin" one. This is just one example of many which refer to these common denominators I've been talking about.

When terms are used in studies, how are we to know exactly what others think the author means? At an American Management Association conference on programed learning held in Los Angeles, Dr. Arthur S. Fleming, President of Oregon State College made the remark that he has noticed the steadily increasing number of new terms and phrases being used by programed learning people. He feels we can carry this to the point where nobody will understand what we are talking about and suggests we try to write in layman's terms. I agree completely with Dr. Fleming. Most of what we write should be geared to the industrial market. I say we, and mean those of us who are involved in industrial training. The clearer and more understandable we can make a presentation or report concerning programed training, the less threatening it sounds to management and the more easily it is understood.

We had a wonderful reception of our first efforts using programed instruction. We began with a commercially avail-

able program simply because it was far more economical
the first time around, and we have no programers. Many
hardware manufacturers are more than willing to either
lend you their equipment for experimental purposes or
else will provide equipment for you at a very low rental.
It presents no problem to experiment in this area for very
little money, and I strongly recommend this as a first approach. By now, much of the ground-work has been dealt
with by thorough experimentation. It is often desirable, however, to demonstrate in-plant the merits of programed instruction. This brings it closest to home. It behooves all
of us to tread very carefully in the area of experimentation
and utilization to insure the brightest future for the entire
technology. We must realize that programed training cannot do everything in the way of training nor is it an answer
to every training problem. To assume it is, and to force
its application in an area where it is not suited, could easily
cause your management to shout "Stop" and thus delay
your activities indefinitely. We know enough, I believe, about
the subject to at least suggest areas where it would not serve
a useful purpose.

And now, at last, to the subject of programer selection
and training. It has amazed me during the past sixteen
months to see how little is being done to determine the
criteria an employer could use if his objective was to hire
instructional programers. I have asked at least twenty people
how they had selected such people, and I have heard at
least twenty different answers. Yet in all cases, those hired
(at least some of them) were doing good work. Our prob-

lem then, was to determine how and if these "some" (both good and poor) were alike. Part of the problem is, of course, that so little is accepted as fact concerning the best method of program construction. How could anyone know, then, what constitutes a good instructional programer? I am confident that some method can be devised to select these people. Although *writing* programs is certainly still an art and not a science, I would hope it will soon be based more and more on scientifically tested and proven techniques.

We cooperated with the University of Southern California in this project. U.S.C. has a very dynamic research group in their business school. The director is A. T. Polin, who is one of the most practical theoreticians I have ever met. Together we decided to construct a questionnaire in which we covered areas of education, personal background, work history, previous training, extra-curricular school activities and a number of other factors. On the questionnaire we asked questions concerning criteria for evaluating the programer's personal background, the psychological and other tests used for selection and/or evaluation, and who would be selected to program—the supervisor of a job, the "doer" of the job, or the trainer of the job. These questionnaires were sent to 200 individuals throughout the world who had working knowledge of programed learning technology. On the bottom of each questionnaire was the question: "Have you ever selected or evaluated a programer?" The responses received were most interesting and indicated, as expected, a wide range of opinions. This was definitely an opinion questionnaire, and we did not consider it in any other fashion. However, the analysis of the responses does indicate some fairly specific areas of agreement and these are certainly worth experimentation and study. In addition those responses which are completely contradictory should certainly be studied and experiments designed to uncover a possible answer. I will discuss the analysis of these questionnaires and some of our conclusions a little later.

In November of last year we decided that since telephone operations were unique in many ways, we would have to program, or have programed, much of our own material. We determined we would attempt to do this internally using our own talents. Immediately of course this required employees to be trained as instructional programers and our problems began.

We first decided on an area of training which would be our initial effort. The one concurred in by our president, on the basis of it being the most in need of improvement, was the area of Customer Representative training. A Customer Representative is a girl who is in our business office and not only handles all calls from the customer concerning service, rates, bills, etc., but also works with the Installer-Repairman in keeping an accurate and up-to-date record and analysis of customer problems. Here is a fantastically complicated job which currently requires four weeks of training for only its initial content. We decided to select personnel who we considered to be the best content experts we had available and who also met *our* criteria for potential programers. We would then train these people in the techniques of programing. To accomplish this we started by getting complete

approval on the project from our president. He then communicated the framework of the project down the lines of
organization. I might state that it is absolutely essential to
gain approval from the top for your initial effort. Otherwise,
problems develop, especially from those who feel threatened
by what you are doing.

Our next step was to meet with the managers of the
Customer Representative forces and discuss with them our
specific needs. We indicated we would like them to name
those people whom they felt were most knowledgeable about
the Customer Representative content. We limited ourselves
to two physical locations and from these two areas, fourteen people were recommended. The problem then was to
select from these fourteen, six potential programers!

Initially, the fourteen were brought together and we
explained what the project was about, what would be expected of them and the impact on the company. Their
questions were answered and they were given a manual
containing reprints of articles pertinent to industrial utilization of programed training, as well as printed data explaining the concept. Various types of hardware were
demonstrated and the meeting was concluded. Each partici-
pant was given a list of the others present and asked to
indicate which five others she would most enjoy working
with in terms of technical competence and compatibility.
They were to return these questionnaires anonymously to
U.S.C. To keep it completely objective according to criteria
established, General Telephone had no direct role in the
actual selection of participants. Each of the fourteen was

then interviewed individually for one hour by Dr. Polin and his associate, Jack Zenger. The emphasis in the interview was on determining how the girls reacted to change, how rigid they were in their thinking, how easily disappointed they were, how they felt about working on the project, their home life and other factors of an emotional and psychological nature such as working under pressure and feelings about intangible rewards. In addition, tests were given them which measured word fluency, verbal reasoning and verbal comprehension, and overall intelligence.

Once these data were analyzed, six girls were selected. Primarily, the six were felt to be tops in knowledge about the job, and in their ability to accept a challenge and use creative thought in working with it. In addition, all were highly motivated people who did not resist change, and who were not rigid in their thinking. They also felt they could get along well together. Our six "astronauts" were given four weeks to get their offices in order so that they could be away for three to four months. On January 29, 1962, the training began and I shall never forget this day.

There is no proven, time-tested way to train instructional programers. Very little formal training has been conducted in this regard and even less on an in-plant basis.

I spent several weeks setting up a very structured eleven-day workshop to be taught by myself and my colleague, Bob Brink. My feeling now: never set up a structured approach; on January 29, I weighed 150 pounds and on February 11, I weighed 142.

I have never been through a more frustrating and, on

the other hand, a more rewarding experience. I won't go into specifically what we covered and in what order, but now I shall deal with some of our conclusions.

1. It only confuses the trainees if you provide a lot of information for them to read before the workshop begins. They then begin, each at a different level of understanding, and they are too full of a lot of terminology which they cannot define.

2. Do not provide *any* reference material or library material for them to read *until* you have covered the points discussed in the material you leave for them. This was especially critical because as I have said previously, each author currently defines terms according to what they mean to him.

3. Permit the trainees to try out as soon as possible what you have taught them. Save theory and any discussion of the psychology involved until they are actually using the techniques covered and can see their own results.

4. Encourage as much discussion as possible. Avoid lectures whenever possible and act as a discussion leader who is learning along with them.

5. Constantly challenge the student by moving through the material at a fast pace to discourage his worrying about his performance, but yet slow enough to assure you that he is progressing satisfactorily.

6. Avoid an eight-hour per day schedule in the workshop. We found that, with proper motivation,

the students would assimilate content very effectively during the evening on their own. In this manner they could review the days' events at their own pace and without their fellow students present. We did have several "live in" periods where three of the students spent the night at a nearby hotel. Frequently they used this time to discuss their programing problems. When writing sequences, you cannot force a programer to set a schedule. When the inspiration comes, that's the time to work. This might occur at 3:00 A.M. rather than between 8:00 A.M.–5:00 P.M.

7. I am certain you realize the importance of reinforcement in a program. Believe me, reinforcement is just as important for the programer. We found that the more we reinforced the student programer, the better her morale and the more confident she became. It was very interesting to note how sensitive the six girls were to equal reinforcement. They resented it when one was praised (in public) more than the other. This even caused tears in two instances!

8. Cooperative activity was most helpful. As practice, we had each trainee program the same content but using whatever technique she wished. After testing their frames on students, this approach was most helpful as it permitted group discussion and critique which greatly benefited everyone. The student is the best judge of a program.

9. We stressed the importance of attaching to their programs a label which gave all necessary informa-

tion in defining exactly what type of student the program was for, prerequisite knowledge required, and a criterion test and other information which would pinpoint the population suited to the program.

10. It is critical to establish the importance of *first* stating your specific behavioral objectives and also preparing a fairly detailed schematic from which to write the program. The schematic should, in effect, be a diagram of the objectives listing the sequence of events needed to reach the terminal behavior desired.

We began with six carefully selected content experts, and in 14 days, not only had they grasped enough of the principles of programing to write a decent program, but they were completely dedicated to the possibilities of using the technology in our company. We now have six programers and can team them with other content experts to continue our work.

The eventual satisfaction more than compensated for the initial frustration, and it was a thrill for us to watch the development of these people and see their tremendous satisfaction as they progressed. Believe me, I learned as much as they did. We feel quite proud of our accomplishment and are convinced we can accomplish even more on our next time around, since we so carefully analyzed this adventure.

For this technology to achieve the highest stature, much research will have to be conducted in the critical field of selecting instructional programers. It stands to reason that

the validity and reliability of any program will be determined by the competence of the programer far more than
by the hardware used.

I would like to conclude by citing some of the data from
the questionnaires mentioned earlier in my talk.

Of the 120 questionnaires returned and analyzed, the
respondents were 50 educators and 70 company-employed
persons. In addition to a comparison of the responses of
these groups, we further divided the responses into two other
groups based on experiences in selecting and evaluating programers. Approximately 41% (49 respondents) had experience in selection and evaluation of working programers.
Credit for this analysis goes to Dr. Polin.

Minimum Level of Education

There was a scattering of opinion. However, about 40%
of the respondents require a college graduate for developing
industrial training programs. This indicates that low-level
jobs will require highly educated employees to program. We
used high school graduates and feel that the amount of
schooling should depend on the job being programed.

Ideal Level of Education and Specialization

Again the college graduate was considered necessary
with three subject areas—Psychology, English and Educa-

tion—being important. Is this perhaps the projection of the background of the respondents?

Extra-Curricular Activities

There were a significant number of responses which indicated this was irrelevant. Such activities as school newspaper, debating teams, dramatics and writing were cited by the group.

Minimum and Desirable Grade Level

Grade level was considered relevant, but responses were scattered between the "B" and "C" level. The "A" student was not held up as the ideal.

Additional Educational Information

Not only was knowledge about the subject area important, but also the ability to write well and experience in handling people.

And so the educational background of the programer should be a college-trained educational psychologist with experience in writing and teaching. If this is so, in-plant programing will be greatly limited by the lack of qualified personnel. As I said before, we used other criteria for selecting our six programers.

How to evaluate a potential programer's job proficiency in the area to be programed.

Here there was a slight preference for giving the individual a trial run. About 50% would like to obtain some evidence of the person's performance by written documentation or personal evaluation.

Who should be the programer—the person who supervises the job, the person who does the job or the person who trains the job holder?

There was a strong preference here for the trainer. Again, perhaps this is a reflection of the respondents' own jobs as many are engaged in a training position.

And so a potential programer should be selected based on previous job performance and a trial run. He should be knowledgeable about the job and also a trainer of the job. It would help if he has had some programing experience and is patient and persistent in performance.

Would you evaluate the programer's personal background?

About one fourth felt a task-oriented person would be best, but a few felt such data would be irrelevant, and more did not know what personal information they would want.

What psychological tests would you use?

More than one third indicated they would use tests, but which ones was not clear. Just as many felt they would not use tests and many felt that a personal interview would be more profitable.

Would you want supervisor or peer ratings of the potential programer?

Thirty percent of the respondents who were experienced in the area felt no need to obtain such information. The highest percentage of responses indicated both types of ratings would be desirable. Those who wanted ratings would like to have a measure of the man's ability to perform on his job, and some indication of how he relates with fellow employees.

What other information would you want in order to evaluate the potential programer?

The most frequent responses indicated that trial and error would show the capable individual. While this would no doubt work, it would be rather costly.

To my knowledge, this has been the first attempt to at least isolate some areas which appear to relate to a programer's success. Much experimentation must be conducted concerning this, and, hopefully, we have supplied some variables to study. Since we know what criteria were used to select our six programers, we shall be able to shed some light in the area and contribute data toward selection criteria. I am interested in Dr. Gagne's reaction to this study.

In concusion I would like to read to you a statement made by one of our six programers which I believe sums up the situation beautifully.

WHAT MAKES A PROGRAMER?

"I wish I knew! Patience, diligence, writing ability, the ability to be interested in a subject forever, tough fingers, complete disregard for physical discomforts and at least a part-time flow of inspiration would be helpful. Certainly the desire to do the job must be strong. An original turn of mind or a creative thought now and then would be invaluable."

"A working knowledge of elementary psychology, a large vocabulary and several sharp pencils are critically required. A large waste basket and several reams of paper will encourage the neophyte programer."

"The freedom to work when the ideas flow, no matter what the hour; the ability to walk away and think or do something else when they don't—these, too, seem essential.

"There must be many other qualities, but these are uppermost in my mind at the moment."

Programed training is a fascinating field and one to which I am dedicated. If I have helped to raise some problems in your minds, then I have been successful today, because so much work needs to be done and all of you can help us advance the technology from an art to more of a science. Good luck and good programing!

DISCUSSION

DR. ROBERT GAGNE: I think that this has been a very interesting and informative paper. It is obvious that Mr. Morse has lived through some critical periods in the establishment of programed training courses, and has displayed good judgment in the selection of people who are going to be programers. I think that his procedure seems to many of us, perhaps, somewhat elaborate. He has perhaps learned something from it which would make it possible to be less elaborate the next time. It is of some considerable significance, I think, that whatever criteria may be used for the selection of programers, the one of outstanding importance in Mr. Morse's own experience is this: choose a person who really knows the subject matter. Some would add "and who is likely to be able to teach it." The fundamental thing, however, is thorough knowledge of the subject, just as is true for good teaching. I get the impression that there is a high degree of agreement on this point among the increasing number of people who are experienced in this business.

I was impressed by the difficulties that were experienced in this project in training programers. I don't know the reason for that. Of course, I would like to point out that people certainly can be snowed under by trying to absorb a great amount of technical material. I think that maybe I might report my own slight experience in this area. I have been working with people in the University of Maryland who have been programing mathematics material. They are subject matter experts, and they know their material very well. They are also highly skilled teachers. When I think back on how on earth they were trained to do this, I don't know that I come up with very much of an answer. We have always started by making an outline. I mean more than an outline, really, because we have made a very careful analysis of the task. Our outline amounts to what I might call the learning structure of the materials to be taught. The kinds of ideas that these people have absorbed about programing are such things as follows: put one idea on a frame, for every frame have in mind what it is you want to accomplish, and try to communicate effectively with the learner. I report this, I think, to emphasis the fact that these particular people have really spent almost no time reading technical material on program writing. I doubt that they have ever read papers by Skinner and others, although they may have. That is all I can tell you about this. I don't really think the training program is such a difficult job, I guess.

Now, I should like to add a word about terminology. Not only is it true that various writers seem to be producing new terms at a rapid rate, but these terms do not always have equivalent meaning. It is also true

want him to achieve each step of the way? Maybe you want to stop and review for a few frames. Maybe you want to take him over the same ground again, or maybe you want to tell him to anticipate something that you are going to talk about later. Maybe you want him to skip over a portion of the material because he knows it already. It seems to me that there are not enough names for all these various kinds of programs. Assigning names to them simply rigidifies some characteristics of programs which had better be left flexible.

Frames themselves, of course, are performing the general function of communicating with the learner. I have suggested elsewhere that one can identify these functions. Frames define new terms, they define goals, they recall previously learned ideas, they guide the learner's thinking, and they provide practice for newly acquired principles. But to try to put these functions together in a framework which is strictly constrained by some external model, like linear or branching, seems to be to me a serious mistake which can only lead to lower program effectiveness. So I would plead for the use of not only fewer terms, but also the use of a more naturalistic language in this whole area. My suggestion is that there is nothing very magical about programing. Basically, it is communicating. Do you want the learner to learn a new word? Say so. Do you want him to practice something? Say so. Do you want to remind him of something? Say so. I believe that despite what may be a trend, much of the current technical language of programing will disappear, because the classifications that are made are of no importance to the behavior being observed.

I would now like to say something a little more general, not only about Mr. Morse's paper, but some other parts of the conference. I think that this has been a most instructive meeting and also a heartening one. I think that we have learned a number of things. First of all, learning programs can be constructed for a variety of subjects that range from simple skills, like micrometer reading, to relatively complex kinds of behavior, like personnel management or troubleshooting. Second, it has been pointed out that the preparation of programs takes a good deal of care and effort, but that it is not a forbiddingly difficult or expensive job. Third, learning programs have been shown to be at least as effective as other kinds of methods, and in some cases, considerably more effective. In certain instances they result in considerable savings in training time, savings in time required away from the job, or other kinds of savings. I think that perhaps we would all agree that these are the kinds of things we might learn from the various reports that have been presented.

It may be worthwhile, if you will just let me take another minute, to say a little bit about what we might hope for in the future. Perhaps I tend to think of this more than certain of us who may be engrossed in the immediate practical problem, but I think we ought to know what to look for as future developments in this area. By the use of these analytic techniques, which have been described and are already available, it should be possible to make learning programs increasingly effective. In all probability, there is a great range of subject matter to which they can apply. I don't think that we yet see exactly what the limits may be in imparting highly complex and highly intellectual knowledge. There are some, you know, who tend to look upon learning programs somewhat as follows: "Oh yes, they will do, you can teach routine things by means of them, and they will probably work out pretty well, but." Well, we don't know what this "but" means or the extent to which we can extend learning programing to cover some kinds of subject matter which are now thought to be very abstract and highly intellectual. I don't think anyone knows the limits of what these things can do. If the effectiveness of programs improves, the day may not be far away when we can indeed obtain perfect achievement of the type mentioned earlier. Already we see that learning programs do a remarkable job for slow learners. Now maybe this can be exploited just a little further to the point where we can truly say that, given enough time, *everybody* can master the knowedge to be imparted.

One of the most important future possibilities to me is that perhaps we can really solve the problem of motivation for learning. There is not much emphasis on this at present. It was, I think, mentioned initially in the early days of programing. Professor Skinner mentioned it in one way or another, as well as other people. Some psychologists believe that the achievement of new ideas can itself be a powerful motivating source, and maybe programs can come to make use of this factor, if indeed it does exist. In the mathematics programs that I have had some connection with, I would like to report to you—and you can evaluate it in any way that you like—that I have seen some programs that I think are exciting. I don't yet know how effective they are, but I think they are exciting. It is this kind of internal motivational effect that programing may have, and that I think possibly we ought to look for and explore to a greater extent than has been done. What, for example, is meant when someone tells us that he was reading a book and he couldn't put it down? How about developing learning programs that people can't put down, because they are so intrinsically exciting? I think this is possible, maybe.

In summary, my reactions are that there has been tremendous progress in putting learning programs to practical use in training, and I hope this progress continues. I hope that we do not set our sights too low.

O'DONNELL: I have one question, Dick. I missed the point. You mentioned cooperative effort during this four-week period. Did I understand you to say that all of these girls worked on the same sequence simultaneously?

MORSE: During the workshop session, we gave them each the same statements of the content on a given subject, and asked them individually to write sequences on this same content. Then they tested their sequences with students, and then we discussed as a group the results of their individual efforts.

MCNAMARA: Bob, I was wondering whether you had any comments on the training of programers. Have you had comparable experience in this area? How about this question of how much psychological background we need to give people, or whether we can forget about it?

GLASER: I don't like to train programers in rigid procedures for frame writing, like writing a frame that has one blank and one response at a time, or writing an intrinsic program which implies a certain format. I suspect that you can communicate certain general principles. They can be learning principles communicated in a common sense way. You can also communicate the technology of getting feedback from a subject, and using his behavior to move him to the next step. The point I am trying to make is that I think you can communicate an attitude, a way of proceeding without using very specific instructions. This is especially true if you have ingenious people, because on the basis of the general instructions, they can proceed and be rather creative. It is like industrial psychology, for example. Industrial psychology is not a specific technique, it is the application of a method and some general principles. My feeling is that we should communicate this sort of attitude as a general principle rather than trying to present any rigid program writing procedure.

I have another point related to your remarks, and it

has come up a few times in the conference. People say that maybe programing is not the thing to use exclusively. You have to use other methods, like lectures, laboratories and so forth. This implies a rigidity, that a program is a specific thing which you read and make responses to. My feeling is that if you take a general meaning of the term programed instruction—as a way of proceeding based on what we know about the student's entering behavior, and designed to help the student reach a goal—then the whole course is programed, whether or not you use laboratories, lectures, or anything like that. A program just does not mean a particular book to fill in.

McNAMARA: I wonder if anybody could comment on the production of programs being comparable to the production of commercial tests. In most cases this is done on a team basis by having a subject matter specialist and a test specialist, You don't try to combine maximum skills in both these areas in one individual, but you have a team effort.

GLASER: I feel there are many parallels between building tests and building programs, aside from the attitude of psychometricians and learning people, who think in different ways. Aside from that, just think of the engineering effort—the idea of the process of trying out the items and revising them, the idea of establishing a validity—there are many parallels. The engineering technology involved in producing a test is very much like that involved in producing a program, aside from, as I say, the underlying different philosophies of the experimentalists and psychometricians. I think that telling people to write linear or extrinsic programs is like telling them to write test items of a certain format without giving them some of the basic ideas of reliability and validity. I think that the parallel is a very good one, and if we could trace the history of testing and see all the things that people did wrong, we might save ourselves a lot of trouble.

Cook: I think that Bob's points are very good. The problem is explicitly to create a factory that generates a certain product. I think there is a difference, however, in the details. When you construct a test and try it out and revise it, and try it out and revise it, you are free at each trial to move to a different group of subjects. When you are working with a program, however, the meaningful test at a later stage of the program can only be performed on people who have gone through the first part of it. This means that you have to design a social system in which the final bottleneck is really the rate at which the subject can eat up frames. You get into a bind if you are not careful. If a program starts to go astray, and you have to stop and go back to revise it a great deal, then the subject who has come with you up to that point in the program is presumably no good any more, because he has been poorly taught. So what you do is that you throw him away and start all over again.

This gets into a lot of stopping and starting behavior, which is very difficult to get out of. The problem is to design a system in which that won't happen.

GLASER: It's like having children. Have four and throw the first two away.

COOK: Exactly. What we have done is to try and buffer this in similar ways. We get a group of people together, we train them in programing, they don't read any literature, they look at other people's programs, and they write frames on a common subject matter, as you pointed out, a very simple one, like how do you get a number from information if it is not listed in the phone book? This can be done in about thirty frames. Just get them to do it. Then sit with them and go over each person's program, frame by frame, in the presence of everyone else. This begins to generate a lot of suggestions. You can't talk programing theory without these frames. You get down to a lot of subtleties, like what do you do with a word "if" or "although"? "Although" is a very dangerous word. "Provided" is an even more dangerous word that very logical people like to use, because "provided" is really an instruction to reverse the order of the two sentences and put in an if/then clause. This is heavy work to ask a single frame to do. You thus get very specific.

Then you move to the programing of subject matter itself. You count on a few subjects that are going to be wasted subjects, that is, you are not going to teach them the whole course, because they are going to be ruined. What will happen is that the programers get feedback. At the same time, they are also outlining the material. Then you can move to another stage where, hopefully, you get subjects that are going to stay with you throughout. In order to safeguard this, you write some frames on one day and test them. Ideally you work around the clock, although it is hard to do. Programers cannot work eight hours a day writing frames. However, if somebody else gets them at night, and then the program writers get their feedback in the morning, they can revise the frames before they continue. Do you see what I mean about a factory? Ideally, programers should test their own frames, but this gets chaotic. At first you have them test their own frames, and then you rotate the load on who in the team tests. Team member A tests one day, and B tests the next day. While you are doing this, you develop a format for the analysis of errors, that is, if a frame generates a mistake, it is not always that frame that has to be revised. You may have to go back and see another frame first, because the frame may reveal something wrong that actually happened earlier. If the team rotates the testing and reporting back to the group every morning, this format gets solidified, and then you revise frames. This means, for example, that you have to have a group period in the morning when everybody is together, so they all receive feedback.

You can also use this group for pretest editing. This

brings up another point. The rate at which you work is the rate at which subjects can go through frames. They can of course go through frames faster than programers can produce them. We have therefore experimented a little bit with what we call parallel programing, which means taking the outline, breaking it up and allocating sections to different programers. This means that you are writing sections that are going to follow sections that you have not seen yet. For this reason, you have to have an editor to insure compatibility. It also means that when we produce these parallel chunks, we have to produce them on carbons so that everybody on the team gets everybody else's work before it hits the test subject. They all run through and make sure that things are compatible, that the points join up, and so on. You need your togetherness hours for that, too.

I am not saying that this is *the* way to do it. I am just saying this is an experiment in designing a whole social system, which will last sometimes for a period up to a couple of months, in which there are a number of critical variables. You have to be careful, because if one of them goes wrong, the whole system can collapse. If feedback is too delayed to the programers, then they are writing what we call "lead frames." They are writing frames ahead of frames that have not yet been tested. If feedback is too delayed, the system can oscillate from one revision to another and begin to swing. It will then go through revision after revision without really converging on a good program. I think that research in the future will bring up this whole social system point of view in which the subject is a key part. It will design the whole system around the rate at which the student moves through the program and try to put in safeguards to make it a stable social system. This is actually a very exciting game to play.

McNamara: I would like to ask Dr. Gagne why these mathematicians of yours who have not written exciting mathematics textbooks in the past now seem to feel that they can write some exciting programs?

Gagne: Well, I think that they are just as convinced as you are that the textbooks they have written in the past are not particularly exciting. Do you mean what makes a program more exciting?

McNamara: What I am saying is, now that they have become excited, could they go back and write an exciting textbook rather than an exciting program? Is there something inherent in a program that causes the student to be unable to put it down, some quality that the textbook does not have?

Gagne: I guess that they would say, and I would say, that there is something about the orderly progression of a learning program, the more or less constant responding of a learning program, and particularly the continual excitement of making new discoveries every step of the way, which does not always get into textbooks. I am not sure that it can.

MCNAMARA: One of the things that you mentioned was continuity. There is no reason why the textbook couldn't have continuity, is there?

GAGNE: That is quite true, but this is what most textbooks do not have.

MCNAMARA: But they could do this. The point that I am making is, aren't we getting around to some of the things that Skinner talked about, such as reinforcement, response, and other factors that affect the learner—which are the critical things—rather than some of these other things that we talk about?

GAGNE: I would not disagree with that. I think maybe so.

SEIDEL: I think what he is asking can really be answered in terms of a statement of equivalence. Yes, this is what a program should be, and vice versa. The exciting textbook would be written like a program. What programing has forced us to do as technical writers and teachers is to focus on the appropriate behavior that we are concerned with. This is what has not been done in the past, despite the long history of education. A comment that was made during the APA meetings last year is that, yes, we as educated people have come through and gone on to various duties in spite of the educational exposure that we might have had. Maybe it is related to the achievement of the poor learners being brought up by the programing material.

GLASER: I think a related factor is that you can get at the behavioral definition of the word exciting. With the program, more so than with a textbook, you look at the subject's behavior and at the stimuli that produced this behavior. You might be able to decide what sort of things are exciting and what sort of behavior on the part of the subject represents excitement.

MCNAMARA: Doesn't this lead us to the fact that we need more experimentation on whether the overt or covert response affects how exciting—if you want to stay with that word—a program is? Or how much the size of the step makes the difference? In other words, what are the major changes required, and what should they be over and above the best written textbook? It seems to me that we still have not answered very many of these questions. Studying the effect of different variables, similar to the ones that John Hughes described this morning, and just not continuing to produce programs as we have up to now, is the thing on which we need continued emphasis. Now that we have started to run, I don't think we should continue to run with just what we have. I think we still have to back up and make more changes than we have made to date.

GAGNE: I am sure this is not the whole answer, but insofar as I have compared textbooks with programs—with what I considered to be good programs—I have noticed that textbooks do not have a really carefully laid out sequence of ideas, if you will pardon my using that word. There may very well be other points to be made, but I have noted this to be true for most textbooks.

McNAMARA: My next question is, if you had a textbook with the sequence of ideas laid out perfectly, would the textbook and what we consider a program then be equivalent?

GAGNE: I think that there would then be only one difference, that is to say, that the learning program requires the learner to make a response after each idea, and the textbook does not. Giving somebody a textbook provides no assurance that he is in fact responding to it. That would be the only difference, or at least the major difference that I see.

SEIDEL: I think, though, that this is a problem. You are posing what I think is an artificial dichotomy. Go back to Aldous Huxley's work on improving movies, the "feelies" and so on. Why do you concentrate on one modality when you define a textbook? Why should it have to be something that is presented visually to the subject? He looks at it and this is it. It could well be that the program is indeed a textbook, and should be a textbook. Maybe the next textbook that you will be dealing with five years from now will consist of a head phone set, along with verbally presented material, various modes of responding, and so on. I think the important thing to consider that we talked about yesterday, and that Jim Deese emphasized, is the analytic power of the programing technique which helps to identify the appropriate factors in good teaching. If there are some characteristics that are given to good teaching by the human being standing up in front of the room as a part of a stimulus complex presented to the student, and if you can vary other factors and show that this one does contribute to good teaching, then indeed you can use it. I don't think that you should concentrate on making dichotomies which may turn out to be semantic ones more than anything else.

HUGHES: I don't think that we are in too much danger of dichotomizing, because it seems that the progress of program writing is going in the direction of taking the program back to the style of the text. In other words, we started with the horizontal format (reading across the top panel and turning pages), and now we have come back to the vertical format in which you read down the page. We are also down to covert responding and implicit responding, in which the blanks are filled in and underscored. So it seems that we are gradually coming back to the traditional form of the text. I don't think therefore that there is any danger of just considering programed instruction on the one hand and the text on the other. I think we are working back in the old direction.

SEIDEL: I think that is a fine approach, but the fact that you can pose this question as a dichotomy, as people have—and certainly here today this has come up— means that we ought to change our focus to consider factors of good teaching or good training with a given criterion in mind and then talk about this, rather than merely a textbook vs. a program.

HUGHES: I think this is what is actually happening.

KNIGHT: I think another term which we can throw in here to boil a lot of this down is simplicity. You need logical order, small steps, and everything else. I think you can see this in one of the best textbook series in the Navy electronics program, which Rider Publications has put out. This comes as close to programed instruction as you will find, except for the blank for responding. I think that it could be converted very quickly into a programed sequence. We would be getting better textbooks if they were written in this fashion.